PENGUIN BUSINESS

THE ART AND SCIENCE OF THE PITCH: THE ULTIMATE PLAYBOOK FOR PITCHING TO PARTNERS, INVESTORS, AND REALITY TV SHOWS

John Aguilar is an award-winning serial entrepreneur, and the creator and host of the business reality show *The Final Pitch*. He is the founder of independent TV production company StreetPark Productions Inc., producer of the long-running real estate and construction show *Philippine Realty TV*, and CEO of Dragon's Nest, a Manila-based venture builder.

His show *The Final Pitch* has successfully funded millions of dollars into Filipino entrepreneurs and the startup ecosystem, and has been a source of education and inspiration for future startups.

John is a seasoned business and motivational speaker, and has given talks on his experiences as an entrepreneur, TV producer, homebuilder, pitching expert, and innovation thinker. He hosts the *Methods to Greatness* podcast, where he interviews Asia's world-class performers, business leaders, and cultural icons.

John holds an undergraduate degree in Bachelor of Science Psychology from Ateneo de Manila University, a master's in Entrepreneurship from the Ateneo de Manila Graduate School of Business, and is an alum of Singularity University in Silicon Valley.

He lives in Manila with his wife and three children.

The Art and Science of the Pitch

The Ultimate Playbook for Pitching to Partners, Investors, and Reality TV Shows

John Aguilar

Creator and Host of CNN Philippines'
The Final Pitch

BUSINESS

An imprint of Penguin Random House

PENGUIN BUSINESS

USA | Canada | UK | Ireland | Australia
New Zealand | India | South Africa | China | Southeast Asia

Penguin Business is part of the Penguin Random House group of companies
whose addresses can be found at global.penguinrandomhouse.com

Published by Penguin Random House SEA Pte Ltd
9, Changi South Street 3, Level 08-01,
Singapore 486361

First published in Penguin Business by Penguin Random House SEA 2022

ISBN 9789814954563

Typeset in Garamond by MAP Systems, Bangalore, India

www.penguin.sg

Contents

For my wife and partner, Monica, for always dreaming with me

How to Read This Book

Like most people, I have probably bombed on more pitches than I would care to remember, or even admit. During my first few years working in network television (TV), my ideas mostly fell flat. 'That's never going to work!' was a common response that I got. They called me 'Mr What If' because I was always trying to come up with something new or crazy: 'What if we make this celebrity rappel upside down the building? Or what if we go on a race across the country and document the entire thing?'

I thought the best path to achieving my ideas would be entrepreneurship. As an entrepreneur, I didn't have to pitch ideas; I could just do whatever I wanted.

Man, was I wrong.

Being an entrepreneur means you are pitching every day to everyone. You are pitching to your employees, your customers, and, if you have one, your significant other. Your ability to keep things together will depend on how you are able to make people believe in your promise, and for you to actually deliver.

In hindsight, growing up in a very entrepreneurial household, I've found this to always be the case. My dad, Dave, was always pitching to my mom, Ellie, whenever he saw a piece of junk he wanted to buy and, eventually, sell in their antique and furniture business. 'You may not see it, but this cabinet is worth hundreds of thousands of pesos!'

Somehow he would convince my mom, and the payoff would come years later when some collector would purchase it for a handsome six-figure sum. My dad would pitch my mom, and my mom would pitch the items to their customers in the store, or whatever pop-up exhibit they would join in their seven-days-a-week work schedule.

My father would later find out that some of his pieces would get resold in auctions for millions. The feelings of regret would always be overridden by the sense of validation that he had an eye for value, and that he once had in his possession a rare antique collectible that he got to proudly display in our home. And to think, the antique and furniture business was just their pivot when their original tailoring business in the 1980s went under. Those junk furniture and collectibles literally put food on our family's table and sent all three of us siblings to school.

Since then, I realized that in order to be a successful entrepreneur, I should also be ready to constantly reinvent myself. That entails being in a position where I am always learning and, in turn, constantly pitching. As I write this book, I am currently preparing to give the biggest pitch of my life so far—that is, to pitch our reality TV show *The Final Pitch* to strategic investors—so that we can grow the impact of our show exponentially. After growing our impact in the Philippines, we are set to scale the show across Southeast Asia and beyond. My team and I are also on the verge of building our very own startups through our venture builder Dragon's Nest, which will require a substantial round of investments into our vision and advocacies. My personal motivation for writing this book is to distil the best practices in the world so we can increase our chances of success in the endeavours we will take on in the coming years. On a broader level, I also wanted this book to be a way that you, as my reader, can pitch effectively—to whomever you are pitching, for whatever purpose or whatever stage of an idea or business. On a deeper level, this book is my love letter to the Philippine startup community.

I share here interviews with people whom I felt would be able to point me in the right direction—world-renowned investors and venture capitalists, successful startup leaders, and communications and pitch deck experts—to find out the secrets, tips and hacks, and hard truths. I also take a deep dive into the efforts of people who have failed time and time again and try to learn from their mistakes. I explore insights gleaned from some of my travels, whether in person or virtually, inside the world's biggest tech companies and ecosystems, from Silicon Valley to Israel to the rising tech hubs of Southeast Asia. It is perhaps fitting that I also share the challenges and triumphs of startups from my own country, the Philippines—a perfect case study of a country with an emerging startup community with boundless opportunities and a plethora of problems it is now poised to solve.

At the end of each chapter, I have also included a few exercises that you can take on as you read this book. They are designed to give you concrete action steps to improve yourself and your pitch. Depending on the stage of your idea or business, there may be some things that may not be relevant, so I encourage you to go to parts that you need, and keep the rest for reference later on, when your idea or startup is more developed, and perhaps ready for the next stage of growth.

I wish I could say that I've gotten this pitching thing down to a science. But most times, I still feel like I don't know what I'm doing. In reality, each pitch is different and is a chance to create something new and exciting, and of value in this world. This book is as much a guide for me as I hope it will be for you.

Now in my second decade as a serial entrepreneur, I've logged in my 10,000 hours of pitching new businesses and concepts—to my wife, clients, team, and the public—in that particular order. I've also heard hundreds of pitches from people trying to make it to *The Final Pitch*. I list down the qualities that have made the people who have gone through the needle's head of our show successful, and if you are so inclined, I'll share with you the secrets of how to effectively pitch on a reality TV show. What makes a pitch good, bad, or amazing? Is it just a matter of having the right key elements? Is charisma overrated?

What you hold in your hands is a pitching playbook where you can try minor tweaks that suit you, all the way to committing to the pitch in lengths that some will probably never be prepared to go to or be willing to take. The pitch is essentially a representation of your story and the clarity of your thoughts. It is, in its barest elements, an equalizer and tool for people to believe in and invest in your vision—whoever you are, whatever you do, and whatever you are pitching.

In the end, I leave you with the final moments just before I attempt to pitch our show as we scale it across Southeast Asia—with lessons from the playbook in tow.

Introduction

Every pitch is a journey. Never is it just a random amalgamation of ideas or concepts that magically make their way into a presentation or a pitch deck. You always have a reason and motivation for pitching something, and the one you are pitching to will always have their own take on that which you are pitching. Every pitch is a call to adventure, and success will always be measured by finding someone willing to trade the comforts of certainty and the everyday, for an odyssey where dangers may lurk but where the rewards and payoff are immense.

To put into context the motivation and the perspective of how I've written this book, allow me to share with you my own journey of putting together our reality show The Final Pitch. *From here, I will introduce concepts that I will later delve deeper into in the succeeding chapters. Call it a teaser, if you will, of the bigger learnings to come. If at some point it feels like a familiar plotline to some movie or story you've heard of before, then that's because it is. The components of the pitch are as much science as they are the art of storytelling, perfected through visuals, timing, tone, and putting yourself in the right place at the right time. Though we have our own unique stories to tell, they can, if executed well, be totally, unapologetically, predictable. And that is not necessarily a bad thing.*

Let me show you why.

9 January 2019. 6:42 a.m. Manila, Philippines—On a helipad high above the country's financial district, I stand face-to-face with ten entrepreneurs who, in a few moments, will be giving the pitch of their lives in the culminating day of a business reality show that was no more than an idea in my head a little over two years ago. As the show's creator and host, midway through delivering my motivational spiel to get them ready to face the show's judges, I, with cameras rolling, all of a sudden, break into tears. The moment was too overwhelming. *The Final Pitch* is, after all, the epitome of my 'why'. I've helped get them this far, and in the next few hours, the 'whys' of these entrepreneurs will lead them to bare their very souls, resulting in multiple investments in the millions. For some, the millions will grow exponentially. For others, the millions will disappear like a sour footnote in time.

I struggled to get my bearings back and, with my voice cracking, managed to deliver my message. 'You are our nation's future. Your success is our success, and I look forward to helping build this nation with you.'

I also secretly just wanted to tell them not to screw this up. After our director yelled 'cut', I breathed a sigh of relief, looked at my production team, and said in what must have been the feeblest voice I had ever mustered, 'You better tell me you got all that because there is no way we're doing a second take.'

That was during the last day of filming for the show's third season, and by the time that season rolled around, we were starting to get the momentum of the show going. It was during this growing success that I couldn't help but think about what it took for us to get here. In fact, almost two years prior, the show almost never happened.

To get a reality show up and running from concept to filming within six months is a gargantuan task. There are a thousand and one moving parts that need to be juggled, and not necessarily in order. One of the first things that we needed to secure was our TV Network. Having been in the TV block timer game (when the producer buys airtime from the TV network and airs their own shows) came with an advantage. I knew what we needed to do. In my mind, there was only one network that would be a perfect fit for the show: CNN Philippines.

I was extremely confident that the network would love the idea. My wife Monica and I met with the CNN Philippines executives armed with a PowerPoint and pitched a concept that was 'a cross between *Shark Tank* and *The Apprentice*'. We were optimistic they would love the show, which, in my mind, ticked all the boxes for a show on a prestigious news channel. Credibility-wise, I've been in this game for fifteen years and have a long-running real estate programme to show for it. I threw down the hammer by saying that the show would be responsible for the birth and growth of so many startups and rising entrepreneurs in the country. We walked away hopeful that we would soon have the country's very first business reality show on none other than CNN Philippines.

After a few days, I received a call from one of the executives. 'We think the show holds promise but'—I could sense the hesitation in his voice—'we think it would be good if we could see a pilot first.'

'Also, we talked it over and . . . ' He paused and took a moment, unsure how to proceed. 'We think the show would probably be better hosted by a tycoon or famous TV host,' he added. I was neither, and we both knew it.

The pain and embarrassment I felt at that time I tried to overcome by saying to myself that I probably would have thought the same if I were in their shoes.

I went through my mental Rolodex of possible broadcast channels, and the pros and cons of each. I ended up reaching out to an old colleague, and we eventually signed a deal for our first season with History Channel, a highly credible channel on its own. Getting the sharks, whom we call 'investor judges' onboard was surprisingly easy and only took a few months. And by April 2017, production for the maiden season went into full swing. The first season was not perfect, but we got it done, and the entrepreneurs of that season walked away with close to a million dollars in funding. Our first season, our minimum viable product, was a success.

The psychic rewards were immense. Producing the show and hosting it myself was deeply rooted in my why. I had, and to this day, have no script; all the things I say on the show are my genuine thoughts and feelings borne from an innate desire to see these entrepreneurs and startups who pitch on the show get the support they need to take their businesses to the next level.

I see myself in each of the entrepreneurs who pitch on the show. When they talk about their struggles and victories, I feel the pain and hope, because I've been there myself many times. Being a serial entrepreneur myself means constantly being a startup. Every few years I would embark on a business spawned by a trend or opportunity I saw. The business would begin from a TV show that I create, but it would eventually be our starting point to start a business in that industry or world.

By the following year, Monica and I made our way back to the CNN Philippines studios.

There we met with the network executives along with their team from production, marketing and programming. They'd seen the show and were quite pleased with what we had done for our first season.

'We've seen your first season and would love to have you onboard,' said the network's Senior Vice President Tek Ramos-Major.

'That's great because last time you said John was probably not the best choice to host the show,' said Monica.

Tek smiled and looking a bit bemused, made her way to the half-open conference room door to lock it shut.

'We just really needed to see a pilot.'

If you compress the story of how we pitched the show to the network, it can be divided into the Three-Act Structure.

Act 1 is the Setup or Introduction.

Here we lay down the groundwork and exposition. We had a great idea or solution to a challenge.

Act 2 is the Confrontation.

It's never an easy journey. We thought our show was going to make the world a better place. As it turns out, the ones we were pitching to had parameters that were outside our immediate sphere of control.

Act 3 is the Resolution.

We persevered and proved ourselves with our minimum viable product.

Victory. In the end, our anguish was assuaged with the words, 'We just really needed to see a pilot.'

Any idea, business, or advocacy worth backing and believing in has gone through some sort of test, validation, and failure. More often than not, you will not be successful on your first pitch. You will go through various iterations and pivots to your product and even your market.

I took the rejection personally, without failing to see things from their perspective. In the end, we successfully pitched the show, but it took the lessons from mounting an entire season to show our proof of concept.

To think, this was only a pitch for our show to be broadcast on our target network. There are hundreds more that we have made, on a daily basis, to keep the show going and successful. This is the reality. You may reach a point where you will accumulate a certain degree of success or track record, and it may get easier. But one thing's for sure: **you never stop pitching**.

In the following chapters, I will reveal to you the three Acts of Pitching:

Act 1 (Chapters 1–3) is the Setup, or 'Nailing the Basics'.

Here we will cover the 'Entrepreneur's Journey', and why it is critical for you to know your 'Why'.

After this introspection we will focus on others—your team, partners, and the audience of your pitch—to be able to effectively frame your narrative.

Act 2 (Chapters 4–7) is the Confrontation, or 'Perfecting your Pitch'. In this part, we enter the belly of the beast, so to speak, by tackling what should go into your pitch (elements), how to use science and art to create your pitch, and the nuances of pitching to different kinds of investors across the world. We also explore here how to conquer one of the most challenging aspects of establishing and pitching a startup: Valuation.

Finally, we end with Act 3 (Chapters 8-11), our Resolution, or 'The Journey Onwards'. As you apply the lessons you've learnt from previous chapters, this section will enrich you with insights from some of the world's foremost entrepreneurial experts, as well as resources you can put to good use. And if joining a reality TV show is on your horizon, I share here, too, how you can shine once you hear those immortal words: 'Lights, camera, action!'

Act 1: Nailing the Basics

Chapter 1: The Entrepreneurial Journey

'If a man knows not which port he sails, no wind is favourable.'
—Seneca

No stretch of the imagination or human condition encapsulates the pitch more succinctly than the entrepreneurial journey. To seize an opportunity and will an idea into a series of actions and processes that result in the creation of a tangible solution is a miracle of the human spirit.

When a new product or service enters the broader public's consciousness, it often means the company has achieved a certain degree of traction and success. If it's a hit, we glamourize the genius of the founder and the brilliant people behind the company. What we don't see lying in their wake are the countless others who tried and failed.

The pitch often is your foot in the door; you get to play, but ultimately what makes you stay and even thrive will be dependent on factors way beyond the pitch. It's important for you to know and own your own entrepreneurial journey, to trace its origins, as it will allow you to home in on what you value as a person and as an entrepreneur. This will enable you to take different paths towards your end game, or at least what you think is your ultimate destination.

In this chapter, I'll share with you the entrepreneurial journey of three entrepreneur contestants on the inaugural season of *The Final*

Pitch. Their stories may differ and so will the results of their pitches, but allow yourself to see as each story culminates, how they will be poised to make their next moves.

Once upon a time, there were three entrepreneurs who decided to set out on a 'quest' to achieve business success—a quest that would bring them together and to the TV screens of the Philippines' viewing public. The way their story ends may not be the happily ever after you would expect.

Story 1: A Culinary Artist's Entrepreneurial Dream

The first entrepreneur hailed from Davao City, located in the country's southernmost island group, Mindanao. Khit Flores, a twenty-seven-year-old culinary school graduate, was pursuing her dream of growing her small three-year-old home-based food processing business. She wanted more, but she was also a painfully shy girl, unsure of who to turn to so she could ask for help in scaling her venture.

And then one day, as she was scrolling through her social media feed, these words, written in an ad for a reality TV show that had 'the making of the Philippines' own *Shark Tank*', struck her.

'Are you ready for the pitch of your life?'

And so it was that in 2017, Khit geared up to venture into a world she almost had no idea about.

She took the first step by filling up an online form and submitting a one-minute video that talked about her startup, Khit's Homemade Products (KHP). The video had no production value. It was shaky phone camera footage of her home commissary and Khit with her hair still dripping, as if she'd just gotten out of the shower, barely audible as she struggled to put into words the kind of guidance she needed as a budding foodpreneur.

A few weeks later, Khit found herself on the set of my show, *The Final Pitch*, pitching to four investors whom she did not know from Adam.

Under different circumstances and with a different set of judges, she probably would not have even made it past the initial screening—except for the fact that one of the investor judges of the maiden season of *The Final Pitch* was Jose 'Jomag' Magsaysay, co-founder of the wildly successful Potato Corner franchise, a popular French fries brand in the Philippines, which has more than 900 branches in the country. He was about to move on from his multi-billion-peso enterprise that, by that time, had expanded to over a thousand branches across the world, and was looking to partner with promising microbusiness entrepreneurs who needed a break.

Apart from Jomag, there were three other investor judges in that maiden season. The first: Henry Lim Bon Liong, chairman and chief executive officer (CEO) of the Sterling Paper Group of Companies, a diversified conglomerate that is into paper products, real estate, agriculture, and business process outsourcing. Coming into the show, Henry wanted to be 'the Softbank to Jack Ma at the time when nobody wanted to give loans to Jack Ma'.

The next investor was Joseph Calata, who, at the time, we referred to as 'the Philippines' youngest self-made billionaire'. He was able to list his company, the Calata Corporation, a few years back, and was one of the fastest rising retailers and distributors of top agro chemical brands nationwide. His sartorial style—who could forget his high slicked back hair?—and movie star good looks made him an easy choice to be a judge on the show.

Rounding out the group was twenty-five-year-old investor Mica Tan. From a casting perspective, having a twenty-five-year old female investor as a judge on a reality TV show is every producer or director's dream. A young successful female investor ticks off the boxes of gender and generational representation. The charming millennial as the foil to the traditional baby boomer? Let's bust out the popcorn. You simply cannot fake an astute business sense, and Mica had this in spades as the young CEO founder of the MFT Group of Companies, a strategic investment firm that primarily invests in family legacy businesses.

To us as producers, Khit had a distinct advantage coming into the show. Apart from her underdog story, she made really, really good meat products. We made sure she had a generous sampling for the investor judges when she pitched, because, as I had described her earlier, she was painfully shy. Her KHP line of sausages and tapas were mouth-wateringly good, and her product samples did much of the talking for her.

To those who are unfamiliar with *The Final Pitch*, think of it as a show that has the best principles we see in reality TV competitions such as *The Voice, The Apprentice,* and *Shark Tank*—but geared toward startups.

On the show, we made it a point to introduce nomenclature that would stick and that we could use for years to come. The entrepreneur hopefuls whom we would shortlist would be invited to an initial pitch to our *investor judges.* The investor judges, with the help of their *investor teams*—members of their internal team who were involved in the due diligence and evaluation process—would then pick four candidates in whom they would like to potentially invest at the end of the season. The picks become official contestants of the show, and are then introduced to mentors who help them in the different aspects of their businesses. This part is the business show version of *The Voice.*

The investor judges then invite their picks to their headquarters, where they issue a business challenge that allows the entrepreneurs to gain insight into the businesses of the investor judges and likewise allows investor judges to gain insight into the character of the entrepreneurs and their ability to work with other people—think *The Apprentice.*

The season culminates with the finale—the final pitch—where the entrepreneurs pitch their businesses for the last time and hope to close the deal of their lives. This part is *Shark Tank,* or its UK counterpart *Dragon's Den.* Only the investors who picked their respective entrepreneurs can make an investment offer. If an entrepreneur was picked by more than one investor, it would be a free-for-all among those who picked the entrepreneur. They can either compete against each other or co-invest in the enterprise.

For the maiden season, we shortlisted a total of twenty-six groups of entrepreneurs to pitch within a span of three days. After pitching, the investor judges then deliberated with their respective investor teams to finalize the lucky four they chose, and these picks collectively chosen by them would then move on to the next round.

We brought the entrepreneurs by batches into an intimate room, where I was joined by the investor judges and where I revealed the ten entrepreneurs who made it to the show.

And shy, shy Khit, who once just dreamt of setting up her own enterprise, was chosen by not just one, but two investor judges—Jomag and Joseph.

Story 2: A Startup Founder's Mentor

In the same way that Khit was painfully shy, contestant Josh Aragon was, well, a natural star.

Well-mannered and poised, Josh has a constant, welcoming smile as he greets everyone he meets. On paper, he had everything going for him. He went to De La Salle University, a highly prestigious school in the Philippines that automatically gives you an enviable network in the local business community. His family's Gotesco Marketing Incorporated supplies industrial pumps and motors to a variety of industries. He was young and single, had a safety net, and was at the perfect time in his life to make mistakes.

In other words, he was the perfect startup founder.

His pitch alongside his co-founders was close to perfect as you could imagine—confident without sounding cocky, with an eager energy that made you want to listen. Josh was eventually picked by Joseph Calata.

Still, no matter how great of a salesperson you are, having a business mentor when you're in the early phases of your startup is a priceless privilege. This was what Josh wanted out of his *The Final Pitch* experience. As the third-generation COO (child of owner) in the family business, he told me as I interviewed him for this book, that he was treated differently when he first tried working there. He was, for all intents and purposes, the future owner of the company, and he felt that employees automatically treated him as if he were already the boss, even if he technically wasn't.

'Also everything was already set up in the company, you just needed to implement,' Josh shared with me. 'It was a very traditional company, and the sales funnel was very traditional: you build a relationship, and you close the deal. It was also very bureaucratic; I had little wiggle room to establish a tech-enabled system.'

There was an obvious lack of challenge working for the company as all systems were already in place. He wanted something more. His father eventually advised him to venture out and do his own thing. This inspired him to put up his startup, and eventually, join the show.

The mentorship aspect of *The Final Pitch* is important because a lot of entrepreneurs still need help. To be totally objective about it, except for Josh and some other more mature startups, most of the ones who pitched during the first season struggled with what they were saying, and, quite frankly, looked sloppy. It was sometimes not so much how they pitched, but the framing of the content and really getting to the core of what they needed to communicate. In some cases, the difference between their initial pitch and their final pitch after going through mentorship was as clear as night and day.

We made sure that the mentors of *The Final Pitch* were people who were successful in their own right, and had the capability to impart frameworks that would help the startups. We brought the contestants to Startup Village, a hybrid incubator and accelerator headed at the time by its founder and chairman Jay Bernardo, my professor at the Ateneo Graduate School of business, where I took my Masters in Entrepreneurship. We brought in the other gurus of the school to join him: turnaround expert Prof. Andy Ferreria, Prof. Mon Jocson, and two mentors who have since passed away—marketing guru Prof. Tommy Lopez, and the guru of gurus, Prof. Ed Morato, Jr, a former dean and professor at the Asian Institute of Management who dedicated his career to entrepreneurship education and consultancy, and developed the Ateneo Graduate School of Business' Master in Entrepreneurship, Master in Corporate Entrepreneurship, and Master in Entrepreneurship in Social Enterprise Development programmes.

We also brought in world-renowned industrial designer Kenneth Cobonpue, and former social entrepreneur co-founder of Hapinoy and Rags2Riches, Senator Bam Aquino.

If there's one thing that Josh appreciated about the mentorship, it's that the mentors were true entrepreneurs themselves, often sharing personal experiences of how they were able to grow their own businesses and brands. Josh recalls one point in particular shared by Prof. Jay, 'The better the fit, the better the value'. That nugget of wisdom reverberates in his head to this day.

Apart from the mentorship, we also wanted to expand the network of the entrepreneurs. Timing would have it that during that month of filming, the Prosperity for All Summit 2017 hosted by the ASEAN Business Advisory Council was being held in Manila. We took the contestants to the Summit and introduced them to Presidential Advisor for Entrepreneurship Joey Concepcion, who was the Council Chairman that year. Joey then introduced the entrepreneurs to people he thought they should meet based on their business interests. It was networking on steroids, and it was exactly what Josh needed in his quest to find mentors to guide him on his startup journey.

Story 3: Crossing Oceans to Face a Business Challenge

Maria Health co-founder and CEO Vincent Lau, the third entrepreneur in this story, went back and forth between Manila and San Francisco during the time he joined the maiden season of *The Final Pitch*. To make matters more challenging, his wife was pregnant at that time.

So, to fulfil his duties both to his family and the startup that he had built, he had no choice but to go on exhausting hopper flights with stops in Guam and Honolulu. Sometimes, he would need to catch the next flight back without even spending twenty-four hours at home in San Francisco. And when he chanced upon red-eye flights to Manila, he would land in the wee hours of the morning and wait in a coffee shop somewhere until call time for filming.

Of all the contestants, Vincent was the one who had the most to gain from his stint on *The Final Pitch*. He was the pick of three investor judges—Jomag, Mica Tan and Henry Lim Bon Liong. Ironically, he also had everything to lose. A nagging thought was his wife telling him before he left that if he didn't land an investment on the show, it was time for him to give up on this startup and get a job.

With too much to lose, he couldn't let his messed-up circadian rhythm from a ton of transpacific flights get the best of him.

He had patiently sat in during the mentorship sessions and participated in two other business challenges of investor judges Mica Tan and Jomag. As the season progressed, he, alongside the other picks of Henry Lim Bon Liong, would gather at the Sterling Place Building, where he would meet with the Chinese-Filipino businessman.

On the show, Vincent's business challenge saw him partner with entrepreneur Jet Cababan of Infusions, a new fruit-infused water product he wanted for Sterling Group to invest in. They were taken to a supermarket where they had to do product sampling and charm people into purchasing the higher priced Doña Maria rice brand.

The challenge was not the walk in the park they initially thought it would be. Vincent and his partner did their best to sell and upsell, and their learnings after the challenge were the soundbites we were looking for.

The whole time, Henry had a team that was observing everything that the entrepreneurs were doing. The whole point of the business challenge was not so much to win as to see how the entrepreneurs conducted themselves. How were they able to assimilate the product information? How did they engage with the customers? Were they fair to their competitors? How did they work with their teammate? The business challenge is all really a real-life and real-time character test. Vincent, despite not being Filipino and not knowing the local language, passed the test with flying colours. His no-nonsense but easygoing nature, coupled with his ability to learn and take away positive points from the experience, gave Henry's team an idea of how he conducts himself outside of his pitch.

As Vincent narrates: One lesson learnt is how to get used to getting rejected left and right, whether it's investors or customers saying I don't like your product, I don't need this. And understanding as entrepreneurs, how to sell.

The End of the Stories and Their Next Chapter

After the mentorship sessions and business challenges, the season culminates with each of the entrepreneurs' final pitch. This was the season finale and everyone's most-awaited moment, where they could walk away with an investment that could potentially set the course for the next phase of their entrepreneurial journey.

Standing Your Ground

Vincent, despite hailing from Silicon Valley, wasn't spared the hard questions—just as he expected. He even had to punch numbers on his phone calculator several times during the Q&A, and, at one point, made a call to one of his advisors as the offer on the table was not something he was prepared for. However, by the end of the pitch, Vincent was able to raise the $300,000 seed funding that his startup needed to help transform healthcare in the Philippines. He didn't need to get that job after all.

These days, Vincent runs Manila-based Maria Health remotely from San Francisco while balancing life with a young family. His company has served over 20,000 members and, at the time of this book's writing, was raising Series A funding with a company pre-money valuation of $8 million. He trusted the process, and was prepared for the hard questions. Now, the pitching for bigger money begins.

The Pivot

As for Khit, she, unfortunately, did not close the deal. Our hearts collectively sank when Jomag begged off from investing in Khit's venture. A few months later as the season ender's episode was being edited, we heard surprising news. Khit had stayed in touch with Jomag and, eventually, convinced him to invest and be her partner. That piece of news made it to the episode and was the fairytale ending we were looking for. Jomag brought in not just capital but his team, too, who flew in to study and improve her operations. They rebranded Khit's Homemade Products to KHP Dabaw, brought in high-grade commissary equipment, and eventually opened a few standalone stores in Davao. I flew in to cut the ribbon at one of the launches of their franchisees' stores.

Sadly, as of this writing, the pandemic completely wiped out Khit's restaurants and kiosks. She is also no longer partners with Jomag.

They had an amicable settlement, and now Khit is trying to expand on her own, pursuing her original business model of supplying to hotels and supermarkets in her province. And, of course, in true entrepreneur fashion, she is optimistic that things will get better when the dust of the pandemic settles.

Selling the Dream

Finally, startup star Josh was able to successfully close a deal for over $100,0000 investment from Joseph Calata during the finale. In the succeeding months after, and as we were airing our first season, Joseph Calata was embroiled in a scandal with the Philippines' Securities and Exchange Commission, which resulted in the subsequent delisting of his company for multiple violations of disclosure rules. Even our little reality TV show took a hit, as we were obliged to air the series that we had shot months prior. 'How could you have Calata on your show?' we were asked. There was no way we could edit him out, as he was part of the cast of the show. We were equally concerned with the possible reputational impact of events that transpired. When the dust cleared, Josh returned the remaining money from Joseph's investment, and they went their separate ways.

Years later, Josh made a successful exit and sold Pushkart.ph to a Nasdaq-listed company. He eventually partnered with Steve Sy, an e-commerce entrepreneur he had met when he attended the Alibaba eFounders Fellowship Programme at the Alibaba Business School campus in Hangzhou, China. They set up operations in Manila for a farm-to-kitchen startup right before the pandemic. Steve had one condition for Josh before they sealed their partnership: 'Don't pitch for one year!' Their new venture, Zagana, grew twenty times during the first year of the pandemic, amid strict lockdowns and, as of this book's writing, has a pre-money valuation of more than USD$20M.

Such is the unpredictable, volatile nature of startups and the startup ecosystem. These three entrepreneurs, representing our show's Exhibit A, tell just three stories of the fate of startups and the different permutations of their business destinies—but they could just as well be seen as the microcosm of the general entrepreneurial ecosystem. These days, startups face even bigger challenges and opportunities post-pandemic, as traditional businesses are constantly being disrupted, work environments are being managed and run across continents, and successful models continue to be replicated in the local context.

If we were to get these entrepreneurs to once again pitch on the show, how different would their pitches be?

I am keenly aware that how pitches are done on our show and how deals are forged do not equate to what happens in real life. In fact, the show is unfair in some ways because pitching in a reality show in front of TV cameras, with the anticipation that thousands if not millions will be able to witness the pitches and deals made or offered, gives everyone the extra motivation to make sure the deal pushes through after the cameras stop rolling. This is a phenomenon I will discuss later in the book.

For now, the next chapters are intended to give you a lay of the land of pitching, and you will discover that there is so much work and thought that needs to be considered before you even make that first slide of your deck. The pitch is an evolution of you as a person, your company, your industry, and the unique ecosystem that you belong to.

But in the beginning, everything must start with your 'why'.

Chapter 2: Knowing Your 'Why' and Finding Your 'Who'

'Keep your dream alive, because one day it just might come true.'

—Jack Ma

It was a calm night in Los Angeles. Roland Ros walked across the vineyard estate where the Philippine Development Foundation (PhilDev) was hosting a fundraising dinner.

His eyes searched for Dado Banatao, renowned tech innovator and the founder of PhilDev. If the situation was any different, Roland would've made a beeline to Dado to strike up a conversation. As an aspiring entrepreneur, he could think of a million things he wanted to discuss with the Silicon Valley venture capitalist.

For one, he would love to consult him about his plans to return to his roots in Manila and set up a business that would create jobs. Having been an exchange student in the Philippines a few years back, he saw the challenges in the country where his parents came from before seeking greener pastures in the United States. He wanted to come back and help in ways he could, to generate jobs and improve the lives of Filipinos. It was his big purpose—the 'why' behind his entrepreneurial efforts.

But if there was anything stopping Roland from approaching Dado that night, it was his duty to usher guests into their designated

14

tables. After all, he was there as a waiter enlisted by his chef brother, who was catering for the event.

Later that evening, when dinner plates had been cleared and desserts devoured, Dado announced one of the highlights of the night: he was offering himself up for auction as a personal advisor. Roland stopped dead in his tracks.

Without hesitation, he approached an aunt sitting on one of the tables to borrow her auction paddle. And right then and there, a table napkin draped on his arm, he started bidding: $500 ... $1,000. But other aspiring mentees wouldn't let up: $2,500 ... $4,000.

It was the opportunity of a lifetime. Roland had no choice but to go all in and bid everything he had in his bank account: $6,000.

'Going once, going twice ... Sold!'

The moment the gavel hit the block marked the start of Roland's journey to become the co-founder of Kumu, the largest streaming app in the Philippines.

Why Your 'Why' Matters

The journey to building a startup from the ground up is anything but dull. And if you're like most founders with the big idea that you think 100 per cent will change the world, I'm sure you're up for the challenge. That is, until you fail miserably and wonder why you even started to begin with. If only tiring days, sleepless nights, and all the heartaches and pains that go with entrepreneurship resulted in assured success, then things would be so much simpler. Fact of the matter is, so many factors have to be just right for you to succeed. Until then, there's one thing you need to know right from the start: Your 'why'.

Why do you want to pursue the business you're building? What makes you connected to the problem you're trying to solve? What is the strong purpose that would make you leave your waiter duties, borrow an auction paddle, and bid for a mentor just like Roland did?

For some, the 'why' is rooted from something deep and personal. For instance, Grab CEO Anthony Tan has always attributed his startup idea to his roots: his great-grandfather was a taxi driver, and his grandfather built an automotive empire in Malaysia. In an interview, Tan said that given his background, he felt that he needed to do something to improve the local transportation sector since a lot of his female friends suffered safety issues when hailing a cab.

For others, the 'why' was something borne out of practicality. For example, Airbnb founders Joe Gebbia and Brian Chesky initially offered their loft as a bed and breakfast because they couldn't afford their rent in San Francisco. During a local design conference that booked up surrounding hotels, they decided to put up air mattresses and accommodate a few guests. Their initial run made them realize the potential in their business idea, pushing them to develop it further.

As illustrated by the examples above, powerful ideas start with a 'why' and being clear about it can make a world of difference once you're neck-deep in establishing your business and growing it. When things don't turn out the way you hope for them to, it will be tempting to quit, give up on your vision, and move on to the next project. But if you know why you're doing what you're doing, you'll remain driven and motivated even at times when the stars don't align.

But the challenge doesn't only lie in carrying on when the journey gets tough. Sometimes, simply taking the leap to build a business is already a challenge in itself.

According to Katrina Rausa Chan, the executive director of IdeaSpace Foundation, which established QBO, a public-private innovation hub and startup platform in the Philippines, many people who have the technical know-how choose not to venture into their own business because they don't have the risk appetite. After all, a business doesn't guarantee a sure paycheck unlike multinational companies that are always on the lookout to hire the best talent.

For many entrepreneurs, merely raising these funds to 'start' a startup can already be an uphill battle. But even with access to capital, the uncertainty of what comes next will still be daunting. What if the product doesn't get traction and the cash runs out even before you get the business off the ground? What if the startup fails and you're left without a job, your life savings drained, and your ego shattered beyond repair?

This is where your 'why' becomes all the more valuable. Being clear about your purpose will give you the courage and fortitude to carry on. And during the first stages of a business, when certainty and assurance are hard to come by, you will need all the audacity you can muster.

SIDEBAR: The 'Why' that People Look For

Mohan Belani, co-founder and CEO of startup and tech ecosystem platform e27, says the founder's purpose is one of the key things he examines during a pitch.

'If you don't have a personal connection to the story, to be honest, it is fairly questionable with respect to what will keep you going when things get tough,' Mohan says.

At a pitching competition in Manila where we were both invited as judges, I noticed how Mohan's line of questioning almost always circles back to the founders' reasons for doing what they are doing.

'I always like to ask founders, "What's the purpose behind you? What drives you to deliver?" If the only thing that drives them is money, success or fame, those can erode easily when the company is in trouble. And companies being in trouble is a very common thing.'

Startups Based on Strong 'Whys'

In my years producing *The Final Pitch* and over my conversations with startups and venture capitalists, I've heard many incredible stories about pitches centred around the founder's 'why' and how it has made the pitch and the startup hard to forget.

Amra Naidoo, co-founder and general partner of early-stage venture capital fund Accelerating Asia told me about one of the most interesting pitches she has ever seen and heard. It's for DeafTawk, a Pakistani-headquartered app that aims to bridge the communication gap between the deaf community and the rest of society.

Now, a mobile app that allows deaf users to talk to people who don't know sign language is a brilliant idea in itself. But how it was presented, and more importantly, who presented it played a big part.

'The founders themselves were quite memorable. There's three of them: the CEO is blind and the CTO and COO are both deaf,' Amra recalls. 'When they come on stage, the CEO is the ears for the CTO. And the CTO is the eyes for the CEO. They'll be working together on stage.'

If you're the investor they're pitching to, you'll know right away that these guys know their market. After all, the founders know the struggles of having a disability, and any solution they come up with is surely worth considering, at the very least.

DeafTawk is one of many examples of entrepreneurs who embody the very pitches they are making. However, sometimes, your 'why' doesn't have to be about who you are; it can be what you've been through, too.

Let's take CEO Warren Leow, for instance. Aside from the business he's managing, Warren also founded Amazing Fables, a small, bootstrapped startup that publishes personalized books for kids. With a few clicks, customers can change the names and illustrations on storybook templates and have it delivered to the young reader. With printing partners in Bangalore, Berlin, Houston, London and Melbourne, the Malaysia-based startup has made storybook heroes out of young people from all over the world without having to hold inventory as the books are printed on demand.

Warren's reason behind the business is quite simple.

'When I was young, I didn't come from a wealthy family,' Warren tells me. 'We didn't really have holidays abroad, and one of the ways for me to really gain insights to the world was through books.'

He wanted to share his passion for stories with the new generation—and even made a way to make kids feel like they're really part of the story.

The founder's personal experience is also important to William Bao Bean, general partner at global venture capital firm SOSV. In fact, it was the very thing that caught his attention during the pitch of Indian startup Phable, an intelligent chronic-disease management app that allows users to manage lifestyle diseases with medical intervention.

SIDEBAR: When a Pitch Gets Personal

Taiwan, August 2019—William Bao Bean sat comfortably in front of the stage in Huashan 1914 Creative Park in Taipei. It was demo day for the seventh batch of startups under MOX, the mobile-only accelerator backed by SOSV where William was a general partner. The hall was full of mentors, investors, media, and invited guests eager to hear pitches from ten new startups.

As attendees found their seats and murmurs settled into a hush, MOX Programme Director TR Harrington got up on stage. 'First of our startups today, I'd like to welcome Sumit and Phable.' The crowd applauded.

Phable CEO Sumit Sinha, looking confident in a white shirt and jeans, addressed the audience. 'Hi everyone, I would start by introducing you to Vir. He was a thirty-five-year-old living in Mumbai.'

The white screen beside Sumit showed a cartoon illustration of a man, the flag of India, and the text, 'Age: thirty-five'. The use of simple illustrations and clipart continued as he told the rest of the story.

Vir worked hard to save up for his wife and two kids. One day, he felt exhausted and short of breath. Upon consulting a doctor, he found out that he had diabetes, hypertension, and high cholesterol. Making lifestyle changes and taking maintenance medicine became imperative. Though he followed the doctor's advice at first, he eventually slipped back to his old habits. And because he didn't manage his disease well, he got hospitalized frequently, spending his savings on medical bills. Later on, he passed away from cardiac issues.

William shifted in his seat. He knew that Sumit was holding off to reveal a 'surprise' somewhere in the story.

From cartoon illustrations, the image on the screen shifted to a photo of two men wearing knee-length *kurtas*—one middle-aged and the other, older, with grey hair.

'Vir was my father. And this is a photo of him taken a few years ago before he passed away,' Sumit said.

'This is not just a story of my dad who couldn't manage his chronic disease. In fact, 80 per cent of people who face a chronic disease face the same challenge.' By the time Sumit got to this part, the audience was hooked.

William relaxed more comfortably with a satisfied smile. Sumit followed MOX's pitch formula—clarity, the 'why', and an element of surprise—and he did it exceedingly well. SOSV ended up joining Phable's seed round.

Our previous examples reiterate that past experiences count when trying to find your 'why'. But 'whys' come in many shapes and sizes. And if you can't find a personal reason to start a project, then maybe you can look for a pragmatic one—a 'why' that you can seize out of present opportunities.

That's what Jojo Flores did when he co-founded Plug and Play, a Silicon Valley-based incubator and accelerator. After a ten-year business stint in Europe, he came to the US in 2005 looking to start another business. But instead of the usual hustle and bustle, he was greeted by abandoned buildings emptied by the tech bubble burst. At a time of massive growth in internet adoption during the late nineties, there came a rapid rise in valuations of US tech companies. But when capital dried up, equities crashed in the early 2000s, pushing many dot-com companies to liquidation.

That could've easily put a damper on Jojo's entrepreneurial spirit, but it didn't. In fact, the situation even sparked a new idea and catapulted him and his business partner to make the most out of what's available.

Stories like Jojo's will make you ponder: what opportunities are available right where you are, right now? Sometimes, all it takes is a creative perspective to spot a situation that could launch a business idea.

SIDEBAR: Taking Inspiration from Present Opportunities

Mountainview, California, 2005—Jojo Flores, who had just landed on the West Coast, was surprised when he drove along Highway 101. The north–south route was quiet and empty, far from how he remembered it a few years ago.

'I don't know what's happening with 101, why is there no traffic?' Jojo said to his business partner Saeed Amidi when they met for coffee.

'You know, Jojo, a lot of people had lost their jobs, around 200,000 to 300,000 people lost their jobs. That accounts for less people on the road, I guess,' Saeed replied.

The roads weren't the only place that was empty. Many buildings in the once hectic region were also sitting abandoned and devoid of tenants. While others saw the situation as a depressing circumstance, Jojo saw beyond the unoccupied buildings gathering dust: his entrepreneurial lenses allowed him to see what could be made out of them.

He researched more about the situation and came across an interesting piece of information that would change the way businesses acquired real estate. He found out that the availability of spaces measuring less than 1,000 square metres was only 5 per cent, whereas there was a 95 per cent availability for spaces that measure more than 1,000 square metres.

In short, the smaller the space you're looking for, the harder it would be for you to find real estate. What was easily available on the market were huge spaces, but small players with limited resources couldn't afford them.

Jojo met up with Saeed to discuss a business idea.

'Maybe we can buy one of these depressed buildings, cut it up into smaller pieces and rent each piece out to a particular market,' Jojo said.

Back then, there wasn't a term for that business model yet. It eventually became known as a co-working space. And the market who rented those small office spaces? They were startups.

Today, Plug and Play has evolved into an early-stage investor, accelerator and corporate innovation platform, and has launched a number of unicorns, including PayPal, Dropbox and Honey.

During my 2019 visit, my view was punctuated by rows and rows of cubicles occupied by startups from across the world, partnered through the Plug and Play ecosystem with different corporations and governments from across the world.

Ikigai: Finding Your 'Why' the Japanese Way

When founder, CEO and investor Chris Peralta was looking to find his purpose, he turned to the Japanese concept of *ikigai*.

Roughly translating to 'reason for being', the concept proposes that for a person to find their purpose or direction in life, they must first identify four key aspects: what they love doing, what they're good at, what the world needs, and what they can be paid for. The point where all these aspects intersect is one's ikigai. Finding their ikigai allows a person to get satisfaction out of their everyday endeavours and feel a sense of meaning and fulfilment in what they do.

In Chris' case, he knew that what he loves doing and what he's good at is building relationships. He also knew that it was something that the world needs because people constantly ask him to make introductions to his network. And was it something he could be paid for? For sure. In fact, building connections has allowed him to close more than a hundred deals for companies like Google, Dropbox, Cisco back when he was in corporate. Factoring in all those components, there was no doubt in his mind that starting incubator and accelerator companies was his ikigai.

According to Chris, applying the concept of ikigai to one's pursuits as a startup founder is essential. First of all, the 'what you love' and 'what you're good at' aspects should show in how well you hone your idea and craft your minimum viable product (MVP). To know if your solution is 'what that the world needs', you need to do a market study and get feedback from your prospective clients and customers.

But perhaps the trickiest box to tick is the fourth—the getting paid part.

'A lot of times, founders don't get paid or get paid minuscule. It's a tough journey for entrepreneurs,' Chris admits. 'A lot of investors don't want all the money to go into salaries. They want to see innovation, research and development. If 90 per cent of the money goes into salaries, they'll just be funding the founder's hobby.'

For entrepreneurs with visions of grandeur who are picturing themselves behind the wheel of a Lamborghini after raising funds, hearing that founders get paid 'minuscule' is a major buzzkill. But don't let that stop you from building your startup. If you work hard and focus on developing the first three components, the fourth one can and will come.

How I Found My 'Why'

Something that you love, you're good at, the world needs, and you can be paid for. Finding the perfect spot where the four intersect may sound intuitively simple, but it's easier said than done.

Getting to my 'why' took some work. The process was deliberate, and took a number of years to get down to the specific words.

When I took my Masters in Entrepreneurship at the Ateneo Graduate School of business a decade ago, I was a bit uncertain of who I really was as an entrepreneur.

My thesis dove deep into the TV industry, which midway through my studies, I shifted to real estate. We produce to this day a real estate TV show called *Philippine Realty TV*, and as part of the business, I was also building houses on the show and documenting the build from the ground up. I called myself a 'method producer', akin to a method actor who gets really deep into a role until he eventually becomes the character.

I was a bit confused about my identity as an entrepreneur. Was I a TV producer or was I a real estate developer? So through the years I built numerous concept homes, got a real estate broker's licence and opened up a brokerage firm, and even wrote a book on how to build homes in the Philippine setting. I thought my business destiny was in real estate, and the TV show was just my way to get there.

A few years later, the graduate school's resident Yoda, the late Dr Ed Morato, would discuss my case with his students. As one of his students, hotelier and developer Gab Perez related to me Professor Morato's words: 'John says since he produces a real estate show, his natural progression is to become a real estate developer himself. I said no. He is not a developer. He is an impresario who puts all these things together to put up a show about an industry. It can be real estate, it can be about anything. But—paradigm shift—what he is really is an impresario.'

A search for the meaning of impresario revealed 'a promoter, showman, someone who organizes or manages public entertainment. A theatrical producer'. Though I had already graduated from that entrepreneurship programme and the words of my late professor were just secondhand information, I was beginning to find clues to who I really was as an entrepreneur.

By this time, I had expanded to a totally different world altogether, the world of startups and investing, with our TV show *The Final Pitch*. I am again going on a parallel journey. If before I was building houses for people, I was now helping through our show startups that would be able to exponentially grow and help millions of people.

Massively Transformative Purpose

My search for my business and entrepreneurial identity eventually led me to realize my higher calling.

As I was already producing *The Final Pitch*, and because of my exposure to startups, I now had an insatiable thirst to learn as much as I could about startups, technology and the future. A sojourn in Silicon Valley led me to Singularity University and to its founder Dr Peter Diamandis. From him I learnt to find my Massively Transformative Purpose. It is by his definition something audaciously big and aspirational, can cause significant transformation to an industry, community, or to the planet. It has a clear 'why' behind the work being done that unites and inspires action.

'The world's biggest problems are the world's biggest opportunities,' he repeated to us over and over again.

He encouraged us to partner with startups and give them access to what we have—assets, brand, cash, customers, data. 'The day before something is a breakthrough, it's a crazy idea. You need to be working with people having crazy ideas.'

In my search for my 'why', I would also stumble upon different explorations of my company's mission and vision. I had gone through Gino Wickman's Entrepreneur Organization System (EOS) Model as well as the Alibaba Global Initiatives Netpreneur Training Programme, both tackling the very foundations of mission, vision, and a company's core values.

From the EOS Model, which originated from the West, I learnt to solidify our company's core values and focus, measuring quarterly, yearly, three-, and ten-year goals, and tackling issues head-on.

From Alibaba in the East, I further learnt to expand my thinking, to imagine the future and the end game of my industry. Most importantly, I saw that one's vision has to have an element of altruism, for it to inspire people to join in my mission.

One thing I realized over these years is that your mission and vision, eventually, can and will change. There is nothing wrong with that, and it is in fact needed as we navigate the constant changes in our industries and even our personal lives.

I eventually found that my mission is 'to empower startups and entrepreneurs to be nation builders'. That is at the core of the things that I have been doing as an entrepreneur the past years and a mission that binds everything that I do. Writing down and knowing your mission by heart seems so simple—after all, it's only made up of a few words—but it is one of the most important and challenging exercises you can do as an entrepreneur. If done right, it will be able to give you the clarity of thought of someone finally able to follow their north star. Decisions big or small can be guided by whether they follow your mission. This book itself is a manifestation of that mission, and one that extends beyond my country and nationality.

As an impresario, the modern theatre has shifted to the TV screen and has now evolved to mobile, and perhaps the 'metaverse'. For my 'why' to evolve, so must I.

Journey or Exit?

Aside from knowing the purpose behind the startup you're building, it's also vital to know from the get-go why you want to build a startup in the first place. Are you in it for the journey or the exit?

Many entrepreneurs see their startup as their child. They brought life to the business idea, spent sleepless nights tending to it, and sacrificed blood, sweat, and tears to make it grow. That being said, many entrepreneurs find it hard to part with the business. Because of the financial, emotional, and mental investment they've put in, they're ready for the long journey as a 'lifestyle business' that will allow them to have the independence and live the life that they are accustomed to, without feeling the need to make it grow much bigger than it already is.

On the other side of the coin, some founders aim to scale the company at an exponential rate as a 'growth business' to eventually sell it or at least majority of their stakes in it. If they play their cards well, the exit will give them a hefty profit and set them up for the rest of their lives, if not until the next venture.

Selling the company doesn't necessarily mean not being as emotionally invested in the business as the first group of founders. Some entrepreneurs even choose to sell because they know that bigger companies will enable the startup to fulfil its larger mission.

No one type of founder is better than the other. In fact, you can start out as a founder who's in it for the exit but end up staying on for the journey, or the other way around. No matter which type you fall under, it's best to be clear with your goals from the start. Doing so will help you hone your pitch better and customize it according to your long-term plan.

Finding Your 'Who'

Knowing your 'why' requires deep introspection, and once you have it covered, it's time to look at external forces to put your idea into action. Whether you're starting a company, pitching an idea, or building a new system, you'll need mentors and a team willing to take on that mission with you.

It might be tempting to keep your idea to yourself at first. After all, you may want to refine the details initially before letting other people in. But never underestimate the benefits of discussing your idea with the right people who could help enrich your perspective. They could, for instance, point out aspects that you didn't consider before, possibly due to an emotional blind spot or lack of domain expertise. Also, working with a team during the initial phase of a project can drive you to work on your idea instead of just sitting on it until such a time when it's not worth developing any more.

A Team That Keeps Your Accountable

One might feel vulnerable sharing their million-dollar idea with other people, but founder and investor Jacqueline van den Ende was glad she once did. She told me how letting other people in not only helped her fine-tune the details of her idea but also pushed her to be focused and accountable.

'What I have learnt about business is that, when I have an idea, I tell other people about it,' Jacqueline tells me. 'And what happens is that some ideas resonate.'

Jacqueline was still a student when she thought of putting up an organization that would connect small businesses in need of talent with students who could take on consultancies for an affordable rate. With such a system, small companies can get fresh views from a diverse group of young academic talents. Students, on the other hand, can gain industry experience and build a professional network. It's a win-win for both parties.

That idea eventually materialized to become De Kleine Consultant, a student-run strategy consulting company headquartered in the Netherlands. But the company might not have seen the light of day if Jacqueline sat on the idea for too long and kept it to herself.

'I met a friend and I told her about the idea for De Kleine Consultant, and I said, well, you should be my co-founder,' Jacqueline recalls. 'That was a good thing, because a month later on, I had started to move on to the next business idea, and the next idea, and so she came back to me and said "Jackie, are we doing this thing?"'

If Jacqueline hadn't enlisted someone to take on the mission with her, she might have lost focus. Having a co-founder compelled her to align her priorities and feel accountable to pursue the project. Driven by collaboration and team effort since its pre-launch, De Kleine Consultant has expanded to fourteen cities and has become one of the biggest student-companies in the Netherlands.

SIDEBAR: Why + Who = Superpowers

Remember Roland Ros, who bid for a mentor in a fundraising event I talked about at the beginning of this chapter? Driven by a strong 'why' and guided by an advisor he bid his life savings for, he, together with his co-founder Rexy Dorado, was able to get their show on the road. But they knew they couldn't do it on their own. They had to complete their 'who'—a team of superheroes, with each contributing a unique superpower.

'We went full-on Avengers. We went looking for Filipino heroes to go back to the Philippines to help us start this company,' Roland told me. 'We went to New York looking for Black Widow. We went to Washington, D.C. looking for Hulks. We searched Silicon Valley, Los Angeles.'

They knew the aspects of the business they needed to cover and searched far and wide to find the perfect person to man each post.

'With the initial class of five heroes, we all quit our jobs, sold our cars, sold our houses, and moved to the Philippines to start Kumu,' he said.

As movie worthy as the story may sound, it was just the beginning of their collective quest. But because their purpose remained unwavering, they were able to onboard a solid team that would have their backs the days when they would go up against the Thanoses that would come their way.

In pursuit of one's 'who', however, some people firmly believe that business and friendship don't mix. True enough, many friendships have soured and have been severed due to disagreements and clashes on the business front. However, Doron Latzer, founder of international law firm Pearl Cohen, believes that you must at least know your potential business partner outside the scope of work before committing to co-found a venture with that person.

'I think it would be very important for you to know your partner for some time and speak not just about work, but see what is his life, his personality or where he comes from, who are his friends,' Doron tells me.

'Being co-founders, it's like a marriage. Ups and downs are bound to come, and you need to know who is the person that you actually want to be a part of . . . It's like a premarital agreement.'

There will be many challenging issues to deal with down the road, and it's crucial to know that your partner wouldn't leave you high and dry in the worst of situations. That said, it pays to think long and hard about who you want to build your business with. Going with Doron's analysis of having a 'premarital agreement', you must revisit a person's background, history, and—most of all—character, before you commit and say 'I do'.

Should You Go into Business with Your Significant Other or Your Family?

The symbolic marriage and premarital agreement we talked about tells a simple lesson: don't go into business with someone whose vision and values don't match your own. But what about getting into business with someone already personally related to you, such as your spouse, significant other, or perhaps other members of your family?

First, let's discuss going into business with family. Some young entrepreneurs who need initial business funding seek help from their parents. However, not all parents are willing to sign a check on the fly even if they have the money to invest.

According to Prof. Enrique Soriano III, who does advisory work related to family succession and business strategy in Asia and the US, even the biggest family conglomerates often have a so-called 'generational divide': the younger generation of the family finds it hard to gain the trust of the business patriarch or matriarch to get investment.

'The biggest issue is that the younger entrepreneurs are pitching, and yet they don't even go to the office at 8 o'clock,' Prof. Eric tells me. 'That level of commitment, that focus. To the older generation, the younger ones haven't even earned their keep yet and now they are pitching another thing. There is a certain level of credibility that the seniors cannot find in the next generation unless the next generation puts in so much time and effort to build that credibility.'

Enrique has helped many family-owned businesses weather the usual storms these enterprises face, and key to this is understanding the principles of governance in this unique type of business setup. As Prof. Eric always tells his clients, 'Take care of the business, and the business will take care of the family'.

To do so, Prof. Eric recommends that family-run businesses put all their terms in writing—through documents such as the Shareholders' Agreement, Code of Conduct, and Family Constitution. In this way, it would be easier for them to manage what he calls the two opposing forces in a family-owned business: entitlement (of the younger generation to the business) and control (of the founder who is having a hard time passing on his hard work to the next generation).

Joshua Aragon, *The Final Pitch* Season One contestant, didn't want to mix family and business. So, even though his family ran a big company and had the resources, he decided to stand on his own two feet.

'I wanted to really venture on my own,' Joshua says. 'My family is very conservative. If they invest and it's not successful, I don't want friction in the family. My dad also told me it's better to get outside investment so that I get to experience what it's like.'

It's one thing to go into business with your parents who have loved you unconditionally since the day you were born. But what about going into business with your significant other? Well, that could be a whole different story.

'What if you break up?' This is what we jokingly asked *The Final Pitch* Season One power couple Mitch Chilson and Sarsi Jonsson, who were pitching two businesses, Fight Shape Gym and Buttr Coffee. 'He gets the gym, I get the coffee,' Sarsi replied without skipping a beat.

In reality, starting a business with your significant other is definitely a major conversation worth having over and over again. If it's not an amicable breakup, how do you continue with the business? The adage of being in business with another person is like being in a marriage rings true.

But what if you are married to your business partner? Patrick and Alex Gentry, married couple and co-founders of Sprout Solutions say it's all about give and take.

'Alex and I think very, very similarly so we don't have big disagreements very often,' Patrick says. 'We've been able to split up the business pretty well.'

According to Patrick, when one feels strongly about one thing, the other gives way.

'But if we both feel strongly about something, then . . . he's the CEO. Period,' Alex tells me, chuckling. 'That's how it works in our marriage, too, and I'm happy that that's how it works. At the end of the day, it's a team thing.'

I know a thing or two about growing a business with a significant other. My wife, Monica, and I started our love and business story in quite an unorthodox way. She was one of my first clients for the first season of my real estate show, *Philippine Realty TV*. As the marketing manager for a real estate development company, she had several projects that we featured on the show, which meant a lot of time working with each other in the professional context, before we even started going out.

In practical terms, we've been working together even before we got together. To this day, she still insists that I winked at her in her office once, but memory is selective when you get past a certain age. The difference in our recollection also goes to show how tricky it would be to tell you about our working relationship without it being coloured by my perspective.

So, for this section, Monica and I answered a list of questions drawn up by our team to offer an impartial perspective of what it's like to work with your spouse.

SIDEBAR: Working With Your Spouse: He Said, She Said

What side of your partner did you discover when you worked together?

John Aguilar (JA): As a client, she was clear with what she wanted. She was generous and caring, but also very conscientious with work. As a supplier to a client, I found her very easy to work with.

Monica Aguilar (MA): One, he's a creative genius. I knew that from the first few times we were going out, but when we started working together in the business, it became more apparent. Two, when we used to go out on dates, he was very decisive, organized and planned. That's the impression I got, until we started working together. At work, he tends to be indecisive, which later on, I realized, came with a creative mind.

What's the best thing about working with your significant other?

JA: Having her with me allows me the breathing room to not take everything seriously. So, if we're out on a meeting, out of town, on a business trip, it allows me to decompress with her. We're able to go on these 'workations', wherein it's a mixed work trip and vacation. That's a very special perk.

MA: I also think that's one of the best things. But apart from that, it makes it easier to be a mother. Because I'm working with my husband and those children are his also (laughs). That makes it easy to pick up and leave and say, 'I need to attend to the children,' whether they're sick or they need to be picked up from school.

What's the hardest thing about working with your significant other?

MA: I'll go first (laughs). I'm a very social person and very open when talking about my life. So sometimes, when I'm frustrated with work, I can't go home to my husband and complain about my boss who wasn't very nice to me today (laughs). So that's a drawback for me.

JA: When my wife and I don't agree about something at work, it's hard not to bring it back home. Because we're always together—at work and at home. In this case, you have to live with it and find a way to resolve the problems within your working relationship as it transitions to your personal relationship.

Was there ever a time when work issues spilt over to your personal relationship? How do you resolve it?

JA and MA: All the time (laugh).

MA: We never fight about money at a personal level, but we always do at work.

JA: And she handles the finances for both the house and the business.

MA: In the office, even if I'm very passionate about something and we have contrasting views, I have no choice but to accept his decision. Because, at the end of the day, he's the CEO and president of the company, and he's overall accountable and liable for the decisions.

JA: We decided from the start that, since I'm the CEO, if we don't come to terms with something major, then I'll make the decision.

What advice can you give someone who is considering working with their significant other?

JA: There has to be a major talk that someone has to be the boss in the business. Because at home, it's the other way around (laughs).

MA: That's not true! (laughs) If you're looking to work with your partner, you would have to look at your relationship first. Does it have a good foundation for you to become business partners? Are you able to communicate openly with each other and settle issues properly? Take a look at your relationship and assess whether it's ready for a working relationship. It's not easy to work together.

JA: If you think marriage is hard, then working with your spouse—especially if you both have strong personalities—that's really taking things to a different level. But if you can hack that and communicate effectively, then there's a chance that it could work.

Though it's easy to advise people to have clear boundaries between work and relationship, I know from personal experience that there can't be a clear-cut line separating those two. It's a constant balancing act, with both personal relationships and business partnerships based on common grounds: trust and communication. And as challenging as the road ahead may be, if you commit to giving your spouse the same respect and esteem you would to any other business partner, then you're already on the path to making it work.

Choosing the Right Mentor

The 'who' doesn't end with finding the right team. You also need a mentor who will guide you, save you from catastrophic mistakes, and help you make better decisions throughout the turbulent journey ahead. Remember the story at the beginning of the chapter when Roland Ros blew out his life savings for a chance to be taken under the wing of his dream mentor? It might sound ridiculous to some, but not for entrepreneurs who understand how crucial it is to find guidance as they traverse an uncertain path.

While 'gurus' across various industries are a-dime-a-dozen these days, it's crucial to be wary of the mentor you choose for yourself. Be wary of self-proclaimed experts who prey on mentees for personal, non-mutual gains. For instance, people who ask for a fee upfront when they haven't even proven their worth yet are a huge red flag. If you encounter someone like this, avoid that person like the plague.

Mentors come in all shapes and sizes, and who you choose depends largely on the type of person and entrepreneur you are. Here are some factors you should consider when looking for a mentor:

- **Skills and experience**
  The right mentor would have enough knowledge and skills to offer valuable advice while giving you allowance to decide on your own. Ideally, your mentor would have domain expertise, or at least, they have gone through a process similar to what you're going through right now. Their field experience would have made them well-connected, and they can use their network to help you out.

  If, for instance, you're working on a health tech startup, it will help a lot if you can find a mentor who has a good grasp of the industry and can guide you through the policies and common practices in the health sector.

- **Honesty**
  Though having a mentor can boost your confidence, you don't need someone who will merely serve as a cheerleader. Instead, you have to find a mentor who won't be afraid to tell you things you don't want to hear if it means saving you from trouble down the road.

Alongside that, your mentor should be sincere about wanting to help you and should not be in it merely for purely personal advantages.

'I think the starting point is, what does the coach want to do? Do they want to show you how much they know or do they have a genuine interest in you succeeding?' TEDx speech coach David Beckett says.

- **Values**

  It will be difficult to see eye-to-eye with someone who doesn't share the same values you hold close to your chest. For instance, MFT Group of Companies CEO Mica Tan says that for her, how a mentor handles work-life balance is just as important as their skills and expertise.

  Take a step back and identify the moral code you adhere to—your non-negotiables. What standards should a person embody for you to look up to them? What moral breaches will cross them off your list? Keep these values in mind when looking for a mentor.

SIDEBAR: A Young Entrepreneur's Mentor Checklist

As someone who used to cut classes when she was thirteen years old to go to the Philippine Stock Exchange and learn how to invest, Mica Tan was already on the lookout for mentors at an early age.

'I wasn't afraid to be rejected, I went around and just opened up myself and said, "Hey, I want to learn this. Can you teach me?" A few said no, many said yes,' Mica recalls.

When she got older and became a full-fledged entrepreneur, Mica didn't approach prospective mentors at random. In fact, she described her selection process as 'results-driven'. First, she would do a lot of research into a person's company and business. Then, she would handpick those who have attained things that she herself didn't have a chance to achieve.

'I wanted to study at Columbia; I didn't get to go to Columbia. I didn't take up Finance. So, these things that I wasn't able to do, I'd look for mentors who could fill in those gaps. I'd look for someone who did go to Columbia or someone who did take up Finance,' she says. 'That was my way of filling the gaps and learning from people in a shorter span of time.'

Aside from a mentor's credentials and expertise, Mica would always consider another aspect—family life.

'When I look for a mentor, I want to know them at work and at home. And my goal is to get to a point where I can be invited to that home and be part of that family,' Mica shares.

'If you're so good at running a certain conglomerate or a bank, I want to see, are you a cool parent at home? Or do your kids hate you because you're stressed out all the time and you take it out on them? It's important to me because my biggest fear is how I'm gonna be as a mom.'

On the other side of the equation, sensible mentors will not take you in as a mentee if your values are not aligned with theirs. BrainSparks CEO and startup coach Artie Lopez says he never works with founders if he senses that there will be a mismatch in principles later on.

'Let's say a founder is more profit-driven than impact-driven. I wouldn't work with them because we would clash when we have economic decisions that would make more money but then affect the environment or the social environment negatively,' Artie says.

This is where your 'why' goes hand-in-hand with your 'who'. Artie advises explaining your 'why' to your potential mentor from the get-go. If it resonates with them, then it could signal the start of a harmonious mentor-mentee relationship.

SIDEBAR: Startup Coach Artie Lopez on How to Get a Mentor

'I hear the same question, "How do you get mentors?" And my answer is always the same—you ask. That's the first hurdle.

You have to talk to the mentors you think you want to learn from and ask them.

'Next, make sure you are not wasting their time. Don't come in not knowing what you're doing, not knowing what to ask. If you're going to talk to a mentor, make sure you have set an agenda.

'You don't need to give your mentor shares of the company off the bat. Honestly, I would say 99 per cent of mentors would be okay to have a cup of coffee at the start. Just sit there with them in a coffee house, buy them coffee and talk to them because the mentors would also want to know if they can help you or not. Most good mentors, most good people, won't take shares in your company if they feel like they can't give you value or if they can't give you too much of their time.'

There are also mentors who are doing it just because they want to see you succeed—no strings attached. For instance, some do it to help boost the industries that could directly or indirectly affect their own businesses. Others are just grateful to be in the position they're in and are ready and willing to pay it forward.

Preparing for Mentorship

Going on a hunt for a mentor can be an exciting task. But before you jump the gun and go on a message-sending spree to potential mentors, it's best to prepare yourself as a mentee first. Yes, being mentored also needs preparation—mentally and emotionally.

First, keep an open mind and be receptive to feedback from people who have been in the space longer than you. As much as you believe in your idea, it would be difficult to develop it further if you don't consider other approaches and perspectives.

'Always be humble, that's number one. Always know that you don't know everything,' venture partner Brian Ngan advises startup founders. 'When I come into a discussion in a room, I come in as a blank slate even if I've gone through a lot. That puts you on the ground level and also makes you listen.'

Second, know what to prepare before you meet your mentor. As Artie advised, make sure you have a clear agenda. Your mentor's time is gold, and it would be a waste if all you're going to ask are questions that Google can answer in five seconds. Sometimes, the very questions you ask paint a picture of how prepared (or unprepared) you are for the meeting.

Last but not least, be accountable for your own learning. A mentor can only offer you guidance and, perhaps, some tools and introductions. Making sure that you acquire the chops isn't their job—it's yours.

Chapter Assignments

Being clear about your 'why' will give you something tangible to hold on to every time you feel lost, exhausted—or both. Working alongside the right 'who', on the other hand, will help turn your idea into reality and fine-tune it through collective efforts. Here are a few exercises to help you know your 'why' and find your 'who'.

- Steve Jobs famously asked John Sculley (who was PepsiCo president at the time), 'Do you want to sell sugar water for the rest of your life or come with me and change the world?' Write down what it is about your 'why' that would compellingly convince people to join you and your mission.
- If you haven't yet, write down your company's mission, vision and core values. Your mission or 'why' should verbalize your core purpose, while your vision should paint a picture of the future that you envision and should align with your mission, with a clear timeline and should be measurable. Your core values are values that not only you as the entrepreneur founder possess but that also resonate with and are shared by your entire organization.
- Imagine you are Nick Fury and you need to assemble your Avengers team. Who among the people you know (or don't know but would like to recruit) would you enlist for what position? On a piece of paper or a mind map app, draw up your startup's initial organizational chart—call them one by one.

- Create a list of potential mentors within and outside your circle. Like Mica Tan, research their achievements and credentials, but don't stop there; find out if you share the same values. Invite your top pick for coffee or go to their place of business to discuss the idea you have in mind. The latter is better since visiting them will also give you insights into their company culture.

John breaks down in front of the entrepreneurs

John discusses his Massively Transformative Purpose with Singularity
University Executive Founder Dr Peter Diamandis

Atty Mark Gorriceta mentors the startups on the legalities of fundraising

The entrepreneurs at the Google Philippines HQ for their mentorship session

Mentorship at the PWC Philippines Office

John briefs the startups on their logistics challenge at the Quad-X
sorting facility

The contestants take a tour of the Mega Global sorting facility

Startups turned flight attendants for a day for the Air Asia
business challenge

John with investor-judge Mikee Romero of Philippines Air Asia and
Tony Fernandez

Chapter 3: What Are They Thinking?

'If you know the enemy and know yourself, you need not fear the result of a hundred battles.'

—Sun Tzu, The Art of War

Knowing your 'why' and finding your 'who' are integral parts of establishing your idea or startup. And once you have those factors in place, the next step is to pitch—whether it's to get your proposal approved, receive funding for your business, or have someone join your team. And if you believe in the saying 'knowing is half the battle', then knowing—or anticipating—how your audience will receive your message is the prep work you need to master.

The audience you're pitching to isn't your enemy, but they can easily feel like so when they're sitting in front of you, looking for every possible loophole in your pitch. In these situations, you'd probably want to know what they're thinking so that you can hit the right notes to hear them say yes.

Ananta Industries CEO and *The Final Pitch* investor judge Michael Dargani admits that when it comes to choosing a startup to back, he doesn't leave everything to logic.

'I'm a numbers guy, I look at numbers a lot, that matters to me,' Michael tells me. 'But it really is so unique and bespoke to each opportunity, taking these factors into account.'

'When it comes to pitches, it comes down to gut feel,' he continues. 'The same way I make business decisions. You try to take all the various surrounding circumstances into account and just try to come up with a magic formula to make sense of it all. There is no one-size-fits-all approach.'

When people trust their gut, they rely on their subconscious to help them decide. Very seldom do we encounter pitches for which the audience will agree to the thing being proposed right off the bat, no questions asked. And if we're honest about it, we might not want that. If your audience doesn't ask questions after your pitch, either they didn't absorb what you just said and are non-committal about it or they've already made up their mind and there's no way for you to change it.

If it's the latter and it sways in your favour then good for you. More often, however, the audience's position will fall short of 100 per cent agreeing to what's being proposed. No matter how excellent your idea is and how well you presented it, your audience will still focus on why it might not work.

In these cases, it's vital to understand their thought process to sharpen your pitch and make the process less unnerving.

Humans are Wired to Look at the Flaw

Imagine yourself staring at a white wall. It's clean and freshly painted. Then, you notice a black ink splotch at the bottom right corner. And, suddenly, that's all you can see. Instead of appreciating metres' worth of chalky white, your eyes are drawn to the desecrating smear. In fact, you may even refer to it now as the stained wall.

No, you're not being a perfectionist or a nitpicker. According to Ben Ampil, a neuroscience and neuro-linguistic programming (NLP) practitioner, you can blame your human brain, specifically your limbic system.

'We have our own negativity bias. If someone does nine good things and one bad thing to you, at the end of the day, you'll only remember the bad thing,' Ben explains. 'Because our brain attracts negativity, when there's a good thing, it repels. When there's an unusual bad thing, it attracts and sticks.'

Having a brain that's programmed to pay more attention to negative stuff may sound harsh, but it's more useful than one would think. In fact, it saved our species thousands of years ago. The brain was wired to immediately spot environmental threats and potential risks so that humans can avoid danger—like being the predator's next meal.

'Our brain is not programmed to look for happiness. Our brain is programmed to keep us alive,' Ben remarks.

This explains why when you pitch an idea, whether in a formal or an informal setting, the person you're talking to will immediately point out potential challenges or possible reasons it might not work. Don't take it personally, because it's not about them being pessimistic or even antagonistic, per se. It's their brain simply performing what millennia of environmental threats programmed it to do in order to survive.

As the human mind looks out for threats to avoid risks to health and safety, an investor's mind does the same during a pitch—it focuses on potential loopholes to help them weed out pitches that may have bigger chances of failing.

Confirmation Bias

The limbic system isn't the only potential culprit behind a tough pitch. Did you know that we have 40 million bits of information coming at us per second? As you read this book, for instance, a dozen sounds could be playing in your background. There are things moving around you, possibly sensed by your peripheral vision. You might be sipping a drink or munching on a snack as you turn the pages. The wind blowing from the vent, the soft cushion you're sitting on, the aftertaste of your coffee. All these are bits of information picked up by your senses.

Amid this regular slew of information, our conscious mind can only process forty bits, so it has to improvise. How? By passing the rest to our subconscious.

'The brainstem is responsible for everything automatic, your heart beating, your lungs breathing, your perspiration. Because our brain is the most energy consumptive organ of the body, it doesn't want to think about things like heart beating—it does those automatically,' Ben says.

One way that our brain helps us make a decision without tiring itself too much is by relying on subconscious information from our values and belief system. This tendency is called confirmation bias. For instance, if you're someone who believes that business acumen comes with age, then you might have a tendency to dismiss any young person who comes to you with a business idea even before they speak. It's your brain performing a shortcut to lighten its load.

In my experience as the showrunner of *The Final Pitch*, I've seen investors gravitate towards pitches that conform with an industry, business, or school of thought they believe in or have experience with. For example, a food franchise mogul may be inclined to invest in a promising cloud kitchen venture while a seasoned real estate developer may be more primed to see the potential in an exciting real estate-related technology. This, however, doesn't mean that investors will automatically say yes to a pitch within their industry, especially if it's a faulty idea in the first place. But because they know the field through and through, their industry experience allows them to weigh the factors and identify ideas with potential and those without.

So, does confirmation bias make it impossible to persuade certain people to agree to your pitch because of their preconceived notions? Possibly. But you can also use confirmation bias to your advantage, as I will discuss in the next section.

Knowing Your Audience

To make confirmation bias work for you, it's crucial to know, first and foremost, what your audience is biased towards. To do that, you have to know who they are and whether they're the right person to pitch to.

Startup founder and IE Business School Madrid visiting professor Mario Berta always tells his students that it's imperative to research your audience before you even set up a meeting. Beyond gauging whether they're a good fit or not, it's also vital to know more about who they are to be able to tailor the pitch to them.

'All of us, we have a key that will allow us to open our hearts pretty much immediately. It's just a matter of finding that key,' Mario Berta tells me.

If you were to use confirmation bias to your advantage, you'd make sure that you know enough of your audience so that you'll have an idea about their thinking process, be on the same page with them, and get your message across effectively. The manner in which you present your idea, such as focusing on certain aspects that would resonate with your audience, is crucial for your pitch to be effective.

Mario recalled a time when he joined *The Final Pitch* where one of the investors was twenty-five-year-old CEO Mica Tan. While other women in business worked hard to earn a seat at the table with men, Mica built her own table; and Mario knew this before he pitched to her.

'Mica Tan, she's a woman in business, very young, very successful. That was the key, right? I think I really caught her attention when she asked me, "Tell me about your team". And I said, "Well, 85 per cent of my team are women". So I remember that being the key for her to really be interested. It was the trigger for the emotional thing.'

When asked about his team, Mario could've mentioned their expertise, credentials or industry experience. However, because he researched who he's pitching to before he got to the room, he highlighted the gender statistics, which imply that his company offers opportunities for women.

Let's get one thing straight, though: there's a line between highlighting the aspects of your pitch that resonate with your audience and embellishing your stories with stone-cold lies. In your goal to be relatable, don't fudge your pitch to the point that you're intentionally fabricating data to deceive your audience. Remember, successful pitching is built on trust, and breaking it is as good as flushing your efforts down the drain.

People Don't Like to Be Sold To

Speaking of trust, a surefire way to break your audiences' trust is to make them feel like you're trying to sell them something from the start. When you're a founder pitching to an investor, it's a given that you want to win their approval of your company, enough for them to offer money for equity. In this case, they pretty much know what to expect the moment they agree to a meeting with you.

However, not all pitches happen in a formal meeting. Easing people into your idea can start almost anywhere. It could be at a professional event or a colleague's party. It can even be in, yes, an elevator. In such cases, there's one important thing you must remember: never hard sell.

'Trust brings the conversation towards more meaningful discussion, and if you start hard selling, it's automatically like a breach of trust,' startup venture advisor Earl Valencia says. 'It's about how you can strike a balance between your objective, which is to sell, and not come off as someone who is actually selling.'

Have you ever been at a shopping centre where the vendor literally comes at you and talks non-stop about the product's benefits and why you should buy one right at that moment? Even if you might consider purchasing the product under a different circumstance, the salesperson's aggressive peddling might turn you off.

In addition to that, the insistence might make you cynical; you'd think, why is this person trying so hard to sell it? Will it go bad in a few days, and the salesperson just wants to dispose of it right away?

According to Earl, the best way to sell is to sincerely look at your audience's needs and offer potential solutions. That may entail presenting options other than what you're selling.

'For example, I want to sell you software. If you ask me to compare mine with a competitor's, I wouldn't care if it's my software you buy or the other person's,' Earl explains. 'I would just want to help you figure it out if you need an honest opinion. You're not pushing your product; you're pushing the solution.'

Presenting other products as a possible solution alongside what you offer might sound counter-intuitive, but it can give your audience the feeling that they're in control of the situation. You're not utterly shoving your product down their throat but it's there if they need it.

'If you're earnest to solve the problem of the person you're talking to, regardless of if it's your project or not, they'll come back to you later on,' Earl says.

FOMO is Real

There are many ways to make your audience want what you're offering without forcing (or begging) them to, and one of these tactics is using their fear of missing out, commonly known as FOMO. Generally speaking, FOMO refers to the anxiety one feels when an exciting or interesting occurrence is happening elsewhere.

Talking about FOMO applied to startups reminds me of the story of how video-streaming app Kumu got one big investor after another because of an element that the founders added to the pitch deck: a photo of their mentor, Dado Banatao, a tech innovator widely regarded as 'The Philippines' Bill Gates'.

'We threw in Dado's face on the deck,' Kumu co-founder Roland Ros tells me. 'The investor said, "Wait, Dado's involved. Can I invest?"'

Dado's reputation was enough to tell the investor that the project was an investment opportunity not to be missed. Not long after, the investor's sibling joined the cap table. Upon hearing that something was cooking, another big conglomerate decided to invest, followed by yet another huge corporation.

Though getting a series of investments wasn't Roland's initial intention, it was, of course, a very welcome development. Additionally, what transpired is a good example of the Parking Lot Strategy.

I first heard about this strategy from Jacqueline van den Ende, a startup founder who has also served as CEO of various companies.

'What you do is you start filling your parking lot with "cars", or the people who have already shown interest,' Jacqueline tells me.

'You start with one car. Then with that one car, you go to the next investor and you say, "Well, Car A was really interested, you know". Then Car B will say, "Oh, that's super interesting, how might

I participate?" And then you go to the next thirty cars. This is how you keep on adding the cars to your parking lot.'

A parking lot full of investors—that could very well be every founder's dream. Subtly giving your audience a hint on who's interested is a great strategy. But don't get overexcited and spread outright falsehoods just to fill the parking spaces. Otherwise, you'd be seen as a sham, and no one would dare pull into your lot now or in the future.

Speaking of the future, another strategy banks on an individual's personal goals and visions for a time yet to come. According to Silicon Valley-based speaker, facilitator and workshop designer Jeffrey Rogers, you can anchor your pitch on FOMO by presenting a tomorrow that your audience would not want to miss out on.

'I think painting a preferred future is pretty critical,' Jeffrey says. 'One that makes the listener something of a hero in the story, so that it's not just one that's about you.'

According to Jeffrey, you need to make the audience feel that what you're pitching isn't only about your company or your product but also about how they can participate in the goal you're trying to achieve—the desired future.

Knowing about your audience's motivations is also critical at this point. Where does your audience want to be five years down the road? Is it the same destination as you're heading to?

This strategy can be applied when pitching not only to investors but also to partners, employees and customers. By sharing your vision with them and letting them know how they can be part of a collective quest to achieve it, you allow them to be a protagonist in the journey.

Controlling Your Narrative and Personal Brand

To urge your audience to join you in the pursuit of a desired future, they need to see you as a hero they'll want to fight alongside.

That means the success or failure of your pitch depends not only on your idea but also on who you are as a person. In fact, many investors

I've spoken with agree that a founder's vision and track record are major factors, especially for early-stage startups that have yet to prove anything with milestones or traction.

You can't control other people's personal opinions about you, but you can, at least, control your narrative—your personal branding.

If anyone knows how crucial personal branding is in today's day and age, it's marketing strategist and millennial broadcast and digital influencer Chelsea Krost. Her LinkedIn Learning course, Learning Personal Branding, ranked twelfth globally on the platform's list of top performing courses in 2020.

'Personal branding is the extension of your personal and professional self. It is both your personal identity and professional identity,' Chelsea tells me. 'When you're in the room, and when you've left the room already, it's what people say about you. You have the opportunity today to define what those people are saying.'

Chelsea says if you don't take the opportunity to define your personal brand, people will make it up for you. So, you might as well find it before somebody else does it for you.

Here are Chelsea's six building blocks to a solid personal brand:

- Personal Brand Foundation
  Chelsea Krost (CK): I like to use this analogy: when you're building a home or a business building, the first thing you do is you start with that solid slab of concrete. You have to build the foundation, because the home will not be levelled otherwise.
- Target Audience
  CK: What do those people value, and what are their needs and pain points? This information is so essential to understanding how to position yourself as the expert, the thought leader.
- Brand Story
  CK: The number one piece to the brand story that I don't think people talk about enough is the breakdown that you've had that gave you the breakthrough that led you to where you

are today. Think of the pitch as the onion; if you peel back the pitch, at the core of that pitch is the story. And does that story connect with the audience, the investor?

- Expertise Package and Design
  CK: How are you packaging your expertise on your website, LinkedIn package? It defines how you package your expertise to the public.
- Thought Leadership
  CK: When we think of daytime TV, we think of Oprah Winfrey, Ellen DeGeneres. So the faces behind the company's brands are so essential for building thought leadership. Published keyword articles, articles on a blog, a website or a Linkedin post, topical live streams or webinars, public speaking engagements, virtual events collaborating with industry experts—all great ways to establish thought leadership or SEO for your name recognition.
- Social Media Community Growth
  CK: Every person who is interested in professional growth should have a LinkedIn presence. If you don't have a website, if you don't have a blog, if you don't have a landing page, your LinkedIn profile acts as that for everybody today.

Paying attention to personal branding means positioning yourself as the right person to offer the solution you're pitching. It also helps you make a good impression before you meet your audience and even long after. By having a solid personal and professional branding anchored on authenticity, you're increasing your chances of getting a 'yes' from your audience—whatever their biases may be.

The Limelight Paradox

Personal branding is critical, and getting yourself out there is definitely a must. That is, until you go overboard.

I sat down with an investor once who was complaining how the founder he invested in was preoccupied with too many speaking engagements. He felt the founder was all over the place, being invited to speak in conferences left and right, and attending more than his fair share of conferences abroad. 'If he's constantly in these goddamn events all the time, who's running his company?' he lamented.

Balance can be tricky. On the one hand, you do want there to be publicity for your business and startup. At certain times the value of this is undeniable. The danger of going to the extreme of this is what I call 'The Limelight Paradox'.

The Limelight Paradox happens when, the more you try to shine the light on yourself, the more you get distracted from doing what it is you are meant to do—running your company. In the process, you endanger your ability to focus on the truly important things, which can lead to extinguishing that light altogether.

Let's face it: the limelight can get addictive. As humans, we are naturally inclined to seek approval. The dopamine kick from seeing the event poster with our picture and name on it or hearing applause from the adoring crowd can be quite the incentive.

I liken the limelight to the fan that directs the oxygen to the flames in a barbecue or a bonfire. For the flames to grow and be sustainable, you need to fan the fire.

This is particularly relevant for high-performing, high-growth startups and companies with a significant user base and stakeholders. Occasionally, your public-customers, shareholders, and fans must be kept abreast of what is going on in the company, what new products you have, significant milestones you've achieved, and what your next moves are.

However, if you have literally just started, you might just be a little candle. Fanning the flames might even risk exhausting it fully. Your focus should, 100 per cent, be on making sure that you are able to do what startups are supposed to be doing—finding product-market fit, generating revenue, and doing your best to weather the small gusts of wind that want to extinguish your sorry excuse for a flame.

Relating this to pitching competitions, I also know of a good number of startup founders who can be seen pitching in all the pitching competitions they can possibly join.

Not to say that you shouldn't be out there, but there have been startups whose main reason for being seems to be to enter pitching competitions.

It's quite disturbing that some startup founders actually make this part of their business model, relying on cash prizes and other incentives from these pitching competitions to tide them over. I found this particularly true for some 'social enterprises' who rely on the winnings from pitch competitions as an integral component of their revenue stream. This was not some casual half-joke. This was actually in their slide deck.

Your enterprise, however, should never rely on pitching competition prize money or grants and must have a sustainable model to begin with.

So the next time you consider an invitation to speak or pitch, it is prudent to ask yourself these three things:

- Will this help me in my company's goals and am I the right person for this?
- Will this give my company and me exposure to the right communities or tribes?
- What is the call to action or result I expect from this?

There is nothing more time-wasting than having to listen to a speaker who is talking about a topic you have no interest in or is not relevant. There are so many shams or pretend gurus out there who dispense advice but, objectively speaking, are not even in a position to speak about a topic they were invited to talk about. Do not be the guy talking about business leadership when you neither own a business nor lead a team.

If you're a startup founder being invited to talk about tech, make sure you are an expert, and not just someone who aspires to build the technology.

Finally, though it's important to inspire people, it's also important to choose to engage in focused activities that will bring you closer to your goals. Roll up those sleeves and get to work. The limelight can come later.

Chapter Assignments

Knowing your audience and how they think will allow you to tailor your pitch for success. In addition, creating a personal brand will help you make a good impression before you even pitch. Here are a few exercises to help you get started on knowing your audience, honing your pitch, and building a personal brand.

- Research about an investor you would want to pitch to. Read their online profiles and review their past interviews. Based on what you've learnt about them, identify their potential confirmation biases. Which parts of your pitch can you highlight to appeal to their subconscious?
- Paying attention to your own cognitive biases will allow you to approach issues from a more objective point of view. Go to crowdfunding sites such as Kickstarter or Wefunder, and check out the projects raising funds. If the proponents of these projects were pitching to you, what loopholes would you point out? Reflect on those and turn to your own business but now with a more objective lens to see if there are issues you can point out.
- When someone searches for your name online, what will they find? Google yourself. If the search results include outdated pages such as old blogs or social media profiles that have become irrelevant (or cringe-worthy), pluck them out of the information superhighway by unpublishing or deleting old accounts or posts that no longer paint a picture of who you are today.
- Build a better search engine result page for your name. Build a good profile on professional networking platforms such as LinkedIn, contribute to reputable websites or media outfits, guest on podcasts and events relevant to your space—position yourself as a thought leader in your industry. Finally, if you don't have one yet, launch your own website. Make each online search result a sturdy building block for your personal brand.

Act 2: Perfecting Your Pitch

Chapter 4: The Elements of a Pitch

Mountain View, CA, November 2015—Sprout founder Patrick Gentry was sitting nervously on a couch in the waiting room of a one-story building. Around him were a few groups of young entrepreneurs huddled in twos or threes, silently rehearsing lines or adding finishing touches to their slides.

The air was thick with tension. And with everyone being minutes away from pitching to a Y Combinator panel, it was perfectly understandable.

Unlike the other founders, however, Patrick didn't have anyone to huddle with. His wife and co-founder, Alex, was stuck in the Philippines due to visa issues. Their workaround was to get Alex on a Skype call during the pitch so that they could still do it as a team. After all, pitching to an accelerator that launched Stripe, Airbnb and Dropbox was the chance of a lifetime. They've heard that only 2 per cent of applicants get invited for an interview, and only half of those interviewees get a slot.

'Patrick Gentry of Sprout?' an attendant asked the room. 'This way please.'

Patrick entered the conference room, greeted the three panellists and set the laptop on the table in front of them. On the screen was Alex, attending the interview from the other side of the world.

Patrick took a deep breath.

'We are Sprout Solutions,' Patrick said. 'We're building HR, payroll, and recruitment for the Philippines.'

Before he could breathe out another word, the panellists started firing out questions.

'Why are you guys building recruitment? That's a race to the bottom,' one said.

Patrick fumbled for the right words. 'Well ... It's something our clients are requesting.'

'There's no differentiation in recruitment software,' a panellist interjected. 'It's done the same all over the world,' another chimed in.

That set the rhythm for the rest of the pitch. It was a back and forth of panellists asking questions, and the husband-and-wife tandem answering the queries and getting back to the pitch deck. It was an interview meant to rattle founders—physically and virtually.

By the end of the pitch, the panellists gave the couple a pat on the back for pulling off an interview with half of the pitching team across the Pacific Ocean.

A few weeks later, they got an email from one of the panellists. They didn't get in.

'That was hard,' Patrick tells me. 'I got wasted that night. I just went on a bender.'

But founders with a mission can't stand down for too long. After getting over the initial shock, they read the email again. And with a clearer perspective, they saw beyond the rejection and found valuable advice.

'For a startup to be successful in its initial phase, it needs to be deep and narrow,' one line in the email said. Patrick and Alex sat down to discuss the feedback and re-evaluated their strategy. It may not be a pitch that got them an investment, but it was a pitch that helped them grow their startup into the company it is today.

What, and to Whom?

Knowing who your audience is and having an idea about how they think can definitely help when you're preparing to pitch, as discussed in the previous chapter.

However, it's crucial to note that there can be no guaranteed success when it comes to pitching. Many of the moving parts involved are beyond your control, and you can only do so much to convince people—assuming they are the people you should be pitching to—to say yes. That being said, it's crucial to take charge of the things that you *can* actually control and that includes the elements that you put into your pitch.

You might not have the opportunity to pitch to a Silicon Valley accelerator like Patrick and Alex had. But one thing's for sure: there's nothing like the experience of making all the mistakes and being really bad at a pitch to knock some sense into you to finally figure out *what* you should pitch, *how* you should pitch, and *to whom*.

In the TV industry, for instance, researchers, brainstormers and producers regularly pitch ideas to executive producers and network executives about ideas and stories to pursue. This is what they do for a living. A long time ago, this was my job. And I sucked at it big time.

The Business of Storytelling

As a young, naive twenty-four year old in 2003, I had my first taste of pitching professionally when I was recruited into the Synergy or Creative Development Group (CDG) of the Philippines' largest TV network at the time, ABS-CBN. They put together a motley crew of seemingly incompatible brainstormers plucked from different universities and split them into small teams in the hope of being able to have them brainstorm for concepts that would change the way the network delivered its content across various platforms. One week we would be asked to come up with concepts for a primetime soap, another week would have us brainstorm for movie concepts for the network's movie production arm, Star Cinema.

CDG was inspired by Disney synergy, a system of orchestrated collaboration where numerous divisions of the company work together to support its franchises. Think *Star Wars* and how you will never be able to escape cross-promotions for a new movie as you will see plugs and promo executions in the entertainment conglomerate's various properties—everything from TV shows to merchandising to theme parks.

ABS-CBN had a very specific market at the time. 'You were catering to the mainstream market which was defined as female, thirty-five and above from the CDE socio-economic class,' shares Mori Rodriguez, who headed the Television CDG at the time and has since transitioned to a different industry.

Mori was talking about the ABCDE socio-economic classification, used by market measurement firms to segmentize the audience. Group A pertains to the wealthiest households and Group E, the poorest ones.

'It was really that game of being able to come up with concepts that the masses can relate to and would patronize,' Mori adds.

I do remember a lot of frustrating brainstorming sessions because I was having a hard time cracking the code. While some of my peers' concepts were being picked up and turned into pilots, mine were falling mostly flat. A number of instances stood out as I was pitching to the executives. I once suggested that perhaps we could have our celebrity rappel upside down from the ABS-CBN building. 'John, are you deaf? We cannot make Piolo Pascual (a Filipino matinee idol) do anything dangerous! It just can't be done!' Another time I pitched a reality show that would be a search for the next big actor or actress, complete with challenges and behind-the-scenes unguarded footage. 'You cannot do that because actors are supposed to be revered and put on a pedestal! They cannot be seen not being glamorous!'

I knew that maybe I was onto something when months later the network's rival GMA-7 had their celebrity actors engaging in extreme stunts in their reality show *Xtra Challenge*. They also launched a new reality talent show called StarStruck that topped the ratings and was an instant hit, forcing ABS-CBN to respond with their own version, *Star Circle Quest*.

Pitching Day

There comes a time in a young person's career when an opportunity presents itself that could possibly be a gamechanger, or perhaps a way to break through the noise of such a large organization. That opportunity came, a couple of months into my job as a concept developer, during the ABS-CBN Pitching Day. The network wanted to farm ingenious, innovative, breakthrough ideas from anyone in the company, and not just the brainstormers who were paid to do this. So the very first pitching day was created for everyone—engineers, editors—whoever you were in the network's ecosystem. The idea could be anything—a brand for ABS-CBN Publishing, a breakthrough innovation for the ABS-CBN Foundation, or even an idea for a new business.

I remember thinking to myself that, finally, I was no longer constrained to limiting parameters. I could unleash my creative juices and show them what the Filipino masses were missing.

There were a number of pitches that got the green light. 'There was this guy who pitched this idea for a male-oriented magazine for Metro Magazine (ABS-CBN's publishing arm),' shares Mori. '*Metro Man* was pitched to the ABS-CBN Publishing executives who were present during pitching day. He was able to talk about the size of the market. There is a huge market for male fashion and well-being that is not being addressed by our current publishing titles. The head of sales was there, the head of publishing, and they all saw the market opportunity.'

I, on the other hand, pitched a new reality show called *The Voyager*, where we would follow the journey of contestants handpicked to embark on a series of challenges around the country. It was an idea that I'd had in my head for a while as I was an avid adventure racer at the time. When an executive asked the difference between what I was pitching and *The Amazing Race*, I couldn't give an answer. 'There has to be something unique, something different with the show you're pitching, otherwise it will just be a copycat of something successful that's already out there,' the executive said as his final piece of advice.

Slowly and sadly, I was realizing that none of my ideas was making any headway.

After another year working in ABS-CBN, I left the network to establish my own production company Streetpark Productions Inc., where I started producing my own independent video content. The prospect of now being free to pursue my ideas on my own was liberating and exhilarating. In 2006, I would come back to ABS-CBN, but this time as an independent block timer, or a producer who buys the airtime from a TV network to air their own content, with its UHF channel Studio23.

The idea for my first TV show, *Dance Idol*, was based on a comment my student intern made when she said that dance was big in schools at the time and there were so many sponsors who were riding the bandwagon. 'That's it!' I remember thinking. There was an obvious demand, and sponsors were willing to back it up. So I decided to join the bandwagon and created the concept for a multi-disciplinary, inter-school reality TV dance competition featuring cheerdance, jazz, street, and an open professional category. *Dance Idol* would involve hundreds of dancers, multiple school and mall tours, culminating in a live auditorium theatre that could fit thousands of people.

I was on top of the world.

That is, until the point when it was actually time to sell, market and produce the series of events and shows. I definitely bit off more than I could chew, and mounting the entire series with my very young team (I was the oldest at twenty-seven) became a logistics nightmare. Half my team were fresh graduates, while the other half were cheerleaders from Miriam College, which was right across my old office. Though I had experience in TV production, none of us had any formal training in events production. You could edit out mistakes in a TV show. For events, however, each mistake piles up and adds to the stress levels of both the audience and the production team exponentially.

After months of mounting dance competitions in malls and schools all over the city, we managed to finish the show's finale held at the Aliw Theatre in Manila. It was a major production and the biggest, most ambitious reality dance competition ever mounted in the country at the time. Few people realized that I was *Dance Idol's* creator, executive producer, host, director, writer, production manager, sales executive, driver, messenger and, at certain points, video editor and cameraman.

Because we weren't able to get enough sponsors and ticket sales fell short, we didn't have enough money to cover all the expenses, including the cash prizes. It took a year for me to pay off all the debts and prizes to the winners. Despite the fulfilment of being able to mount such an impressive show, it was also the lowest point in my young life, as my creation was not financially viable. I grew up fast that year. I swore it would never happen again.

Why My Pitches and Concepts Didn't Work

My failed pitches in my early TV career clearly showed an inability to see the market. I was focused too much on pitching what I wanted to do and what I was passionate about, without seeing the needs of my 'clients'—the network executives who had very clear expectations and target demographics. I used to despise the fact that these executives never veered too far away from their formulaic perception of what they felt the masses needed and were looking for, but becoming an entrepreneur myself later on, I finally understood why they wanted to minimize risks to protect the network's bottom line that had so many people relying on its continued viability and profitability.

Most times when I did have good ideas and they would not fly, I now know that I was just barking up the wrong tree. *What* to pitch *to whom* is as important as the concept itself. Hindsight is always twenty-twenty.

When I finally set sail on my own ship, I set out to create something from a mere tip, without doing extensive research on the industry and the potential market size. Perhaps things could have turned out different financially for *Dance Idol* if I had a more experienced salesperson or team onboard helping me instead of me trying to do everything myself. I've always aspired to think big, and perhaps a bit of hubris came into play—having a very big chip on my shoulder made me punch way above my weight class—and made me mount something I was totally unprepared for. Would I have changed anything if I had the chance knowing what I know now? Absolutely not.

I've always said to people that every rejection I've got and every mistake I've made has made me stronger, wiser and better. All these mistakes and learning from first-hand experience are truly better than any book I've read.

Immediately after *Dance Idol*, I pivoted and saw a growing trend in the real estate market in the Philippines in 2007. Being an avid newspaper reader, I noticed there were so many full-page real estate ads in the papers. This was clearly a huge market for print advertising. How come there was no show on real estate on TV?

That year I had planned a long overdue trip to visit my sister in Canada, and I had asked my new sales executive—my only full-time employee at the time since I had just finished paying off all my debts— to compile a list of all real estate developers in the Philippines. I had also used the trip to do a little bit of first-hand informal focus group discussions with relatives and their friends, Filipinos who belonged to the diaspora with dreams of one day coming back home to the Philippines to retire.

They belonged to the target market of all of these real estate developers. They all agreed that they would definitely watch a show that would take people on a virtual tour of the projects of the developers back home, since they themselves could not do it.

The following year, I came back to ABS-CBN, and worked out a block time deal for a slot on the ABS-CBN News Channel (ANC)- which, incidentally, was also being aired globally on The Filipino Channel, and available to Filipinos across the world. We produced 'the country's first real estate TV show for the local and global Filipino audience', *Philippine Realty TV*.

It started off rocky at first. In our first season, we were able to get two real estate developers who were early adopters of our format. But apart from the developers, there were hundreds of untapped prospective clients that belonged to the construction supplies industry that were open to advertising on TV. The problem was, they didn't have any advertising budget but were willing to pay us in barter or products in exchange for advertising.

The lightbulb moment came when I had a conversation with my mother one night after dinner. I produce a real estate show, and yet I don't have my own house. What if I build my first home on the show? 'Why not?' she casually says. This is what started me off on our show's unique business model of getting paid in products and using these to build homes that we would later sell for profit.

We've successfully managed to carve a unique niche with our show, building concept homes from my own Project: First Home, the green and sustainable Project: Green Home, the flood and climate adaptive Project: Smart Home that features a floatable carport, and the tech-enabled, fully automated Project: Smart Home 2.0. At the time of writing this book, we were celebrating our twentieth season on air, on CNN Philippines, our home network since the fifteenth season.

If you're reading this book in the hopes of not making mistakes, I'm telling you now that you're missing the whole point. Pitching is all about crazy ideas, making mistakes, getting rejected, and pivoting and recreating yourself. That is what builds your character and is what gives you the clear and deep level of insight you will never get from someone else's experience.

There is no better mentor than the pain of failure, and no greater microscope than your own tears.

How: Types of Pitches to Master

Now that I've shared with you examples of why I was just so bad and the value of knowing *what* to pitch and *to whom*, it is probably a good time to talk about frameworks to give you some headway on *how* to craft your pitch. We'll be getting very specific, so buckle up.

Knowing what your clients want, which in my case were network executives and sponsors, will help you customize your pitch and gear it better for success.

'It's not that founders are not prepared, but they do the wrong preparation,' *Pitch To Win* author and TEDx speech coach David Beckett tells me. According to David, knowing who you're pitching to should be part and parcel of your preparation.

'For example, they might not have scouted, "Is this the right investor for me? What is this investor interested in? Why are they talking to me? And what do they care about? What do I want these people to do?"'

But before we talk about customizing your pitch, let's discuss the types of pitches and the elements to include in your proposal. Throughout the course of your project, you'll probably be pitching to a number of people—investors, potential partners, customers and many others. Here are some of the pitches you need to master as you build and pitch yourself and your business.

1.   Elevator pitch

An elevator pitch is basically a short summary of who you are and what you do, and something that you do to brief someone about an idea and spark their interest while you're at it. It's called so because it must be succinct enough to deliver during an elevator ride.

Think of it this way: You go in an elevator car and just before the doors close, a potential investor hops in and presses the number eight. You exchange pleasantries. If you were to go for the opportunity, you would need to pitch your business idea before the car reaches the eighth floor. That falls somewhere between 20 seconds to one minute.

When a product pitches itself

Most elevator pitches are delivered through a casual conversation. Other times, it can even be as short and simple as showing someone what you've built and letting that thing speak for itself.

For instance, Foxmont Capital Partners managing partner Franco Varona considers Roland Ros' pitch to him as an elevator pitch. Roland, whom I have mentioned in previous chapters, is the co-founder of Kumu, a community streaming platform where users can get paid by becoming a livestreamer or win cash prizes by playing live games.

'It was not even actually a pitch; that's the really nice thing about it,' Franco tells me. 'It was them coming to meet us just to get to know us. They're new in town and they're actually already funded, they have angel investors. . . . And then Roland did one simple thing: He whipped out his product, showed us a livestreamer, clicked a Malacañang virtual gift, which I think was worth P5,000 ($100). He gave it to a livestreamer, and we all just watched that livestreamer freak out and almost cry.'

Roland already knew that showing the impact of his product would be much more convincing than any spiel he could ever deliver in a short amount of time.

'At that point, I was already reaching out to my wallet and saying, "Okay, please, can you just kick out one of your angel investors?"' Franco recalls, chuckling.

Tweet Pitch: The Modern Elevator Pitch

The elevator pitch may mean different things to different people, but one thing's for sure: It's short and succinct. In the new normal where people have shifted to digital for almost all forms of communication, the traditional elevator pitch has evolved into a new form—the tweet pitch.

Also called a 'twit' pitch, this type of one-line pitch proposes an idea in 140 characters, or the original length of a Twitter post before the platform expanded its character limitation to 280 characters.

You're not going to actually tweet your 140-character pitch to an investor. Instead, this one-line composition is meant to explain your business on sites where it will be listed, such as LinkedIn, CrunchBase, AngelList, and other websites for competitions, accelerators, and crowdfunding.

Your tweet allows you to make an impression in a few seconds. Whether you reel in your audience or make them hit the 'close window' button is entirely up to those 140 characters.

As for the actual elevator pitch that's delivered face-to-face, it doesn't have to be as nerve-wracking and rehearsed as some people may imagine it to be. I know because I do it constantly. Sometimes, without even being aware of it.

SIDEBAR: Elevator Pitching a TV Show

As my wife, Monica, and I entered the main ballroom of the Manila Polo Club, I quickly scanned the guest list, and it was clear that this was no ordinary event. There were approximately 300 of the country's elite from government and business. Tycoons, past presidents, captains of industry. It was organized by GoNegosyo, a non-profit organization that advocates for a change in the nation's mindset and attitude, spearheaded by Presidential Advisor for Entrepreneurship Joey Concepcion.

The main thrust of the movement is to raise awareness and give people access to the three Ms: Money, Market, Mentorship. In a developing country such as the Philippines, the three Ms are extremely difficult to come by if no form of support from a 'big brother' is available. And the event that night was meant for business and industry leaders to come together to rally behind a common objective of providing our fellow Filipino entrepreneurs with the much-needed resources they would need—whether it was in the form of access to capital, customers, or perhaps linkages to organizations or individuals who could directly help them with their business challenges.

To be honest, I didn't exactly know how Monica and I fit in that night. Were we there to receive support or give it? A tremendous sense of imposter syndrome definitely enveloped me. But in a room this diverse, people have reached the peaks of success from every imaginable beginning you could possibly think of.

At some point, I told Monica how fortunate we were to be in this room; we could practically go to anyone we felt we wanted to meet to pitch an idea or business or partnership to. At that moment it hit me. 'Remember *Shark Tank*?' I asked Monica. We'd been binge-watching the show for a few weeks with the kids, prompting me to tell Monica one night, as I always do when I think of possible ideas for shows we could produce, that we should come up with our own version. 'I think we should do it now.'

'Yes, I think so, too,' she said. At that precise moment, *The Final Pitch* was conceived. And that's all I needed to get to work.

I immediately scanned the room to see who we could possibly pitch this show to. In my mind, I just wanted to talk about the idea, validate it, and see how people would react. Would people have a positive or negative reaction to it? Could there be a potential judge for the show at this very event? I ended up talking about the show's core idea to a few people.

This was my spiel:

Are you familiar with *Shark Tank*? (person responds)

If no, explain what Shark Tank is.

If yes, proceed with:

We're coming up with our own version for the Philippines.

My elevator pitch was that simple. The rest of the time was spent mentally taking note of what they said after that. If they were familiar with *Shark Tank*, common responses would revolve around them agreeing that the Philippines needs its own version, and that entrepreneurship is not something that comes naturally to Filipinos and the *Shark Tank* format would be a good way to get more people to think about entrepreneurship. I would then close with, 'Maybe we can discuss further and see how we can work together on it in the future'. There would be an exchange of cards, and a promise to stay in touch after the event.

The fact that one of the people whom I met and talked to at the event eventually came onboard to join us for the filming of our maiden season as one of the investor judges six months later was pure dumb luck. Or was it?

To add to that, Joey Concepcion also eventually became a mentor on our first season.

My objective for telling people about the idea (even if I had just thought about it a few minutes earlier) was really to solicit a reaction and feedback. It was a way to open up a conversation so we could discuss the show later on to explore how we could work together—and we did just that.

2. Short-form pitch

An elevator pitch may be seen as an ice breaker, a brief opportunity to get your idea out in front of your audience. But the reason it's so important is that a successful elevator pitch can help you land an opportunity for a short-form pitch.

A short-form pitch allows for a longer time to tell your company's story—around ten minutes. Remember the pitch that Patrick and

Alex Gentry did for Y Combinator I mentioned at the beginning of this chapter? That could be considered a short-form pitch.

On *The Final Pitch*, we give our contestants exactly ten minutes to give their pitch in front of the investors. Within that span of time, they should have communicated everything about their startup or business, and be prepared for questions after.

Other platforms allow more or less the same amount of time. For example, Cradle Fund, Malaysia's early-stage startup venture fund, allots a shorter allowance for the initial pitch but offers more time to accommodate panellists' queries.

'Once they come in, it's five minutes, pitch; ten minutes, question and answer. All in all, 15 minutes,' Adam Ramskay, Cradle's head of unit for strategy says. 'In front of the panel of three to five people maximum, but usually, it's three people.'

Given that amount of time with your audience, what would you tell them to get them interested? For sure, you'll want to focus on the most important aspects of your idea or business. Its purpose, the people behind it—aspects that will help catch sponsors and customers hook, line and sinker. We'll discuss each element in detail in the next section.

3.   Long-form pitch

If you're successful during the short-form pitch, your audience will, hopefully, invite you for a long-form pitch. Unlike the former, which is basically an introduction to your business, the latter discusses the nitty-gritty of your idea.

'These startups that we feel have a better potential to scale and to grow, we'll call them in to understand more of their business,' Adam shares with me. 'Because the five minutes don't really give justice to them, their business. So, we call them in and once we've understood more of their business, then we'll take them out to the investment committee.'

At this point, your audience is more or less already interested in your company and offering more detailed information will allow them to gauge if they really want to sign on the dotted line.

The elements that you include in your pitch may vary depending on how developed your idea is, or at what stage you're in. For example, if you're a startup founder raising for seed funding, your pitch deck would probably have fewer slides compared to when you've been around for some time and you're already raising for Series A.[1] I'll also discuss the elements you may want to include in your long-form pitch over the next section.

Elements of the Pitch: The Essentials

Now that we've discussed the types of pitches to master, it's time to tackle the elements that you need to include in each. By now, every startup worth their salt knows Guy Kawasaki's ten slides. These are the ten common, recommended slides every pitch deck must have. There are some who swear by this and would not deviate from this tried and tested formula. But, as I've mentioned earlier, the set of elements you include in your pitch depends on your idea and where you are in your journey.

'The idea of the ten-slide deck is not a set-in-stone method. Somebody is not going to kick you out because you have twelve slides. If they kick you out, then you shouldn't be presenting to them,' Ashley Smithers, award-winning graphic designer, tells me.

Ashley is the founder and principal of 1821 Designs, a creative firm that specializes in presentation design and keynote direction for public and private companies. 'It's not about ten slides, it's about pieces of information that people would digest. And if you take that

---

[1] Most startups grow their business by raising capital through external funding. Investors put money into the company in exchange for partial ownership or equity of that company. Early-stage startups usually begin with seed funding from angel investors, hence the alternative term angel funding. As the company needs more capital as it grows, founders will have to raise for further funding. These funding rounds are called Series A, B, C, and so on. The letters corresponding to funding amounts can vary per territory or region. According to Leticia Souza, vice president of finance at Uploan.ph, during Series A, a company is usually valued at least $10 million in Asia and Latin America. However, this value can vary depending on numerous factors, such as the investment environment and founder reputation.

and link it together with people, you make it into a real story that has a consistency,' Ashley explains.

In this section, we will go in-depth into pieces of information you should include in your pitch and go over nuggets of wisdom from founders, investors and business experts I've talked with while writing this book.

The first three elements are the essential parts of a pitch. Whether you're an employee pitching a new system to the higher-ups or a founder pitching for pre-seed funding, these are the must-have elements to include. **These are the elements that tell your audience what you're pitching, why you're pitching it, and what you want them to do about it. Without all of these three present, your pitch will either be irrelevant, incoherent or just plain confusing.**

'Create a pitch that even your grandmother would understand,' CEO and investor Chris Peralta advises.

Startup founders, in particular, may feel the need to over-explain details. But there's a proper time for that, and it's not during the first pitch.

'Once you get in more talks with the venture capitalist (VC), they're going to do their due diligence. The VC analysts are going to start asking all the tough and technical questions anyway, but in the beginning, your pitch needs to be crisp, relatable. Try to ignite an emotional connection with the audience,' Chris adds.

1.   The Problem or Opportunity

If you're starting your pitch by putting the spotlight on your product or idea, you're missing the whole point. Pitching is all about storytelling and one of the simplest forms of telling a story is through a linear narrative. Begin your pitch with the issue or situation that pushed you to come up with your idea in the first place.

'I think that the best pitch always starts with the problem you solve,' *Pitch To Win* author and TEDx speech coach David Beckett advises. 'Why are you doing this? Why did you create it? Nobody buys something just because you created it. They buy it because it solves a problem or helps them do something better.'

Stating the problem doesn't need to be complicated. You can express it in the form of a short story or an anecdote. For instance, Chris told me about a startup that caught his attention by starting with a simple opening line. The founder was pitching a system that would maximize the efficiency of trucking operations, making sure that each trailer is loaded to and from the parking facility.

'He described it in his pitch by asking, "Did anyone drive to this demo day today? Did anyone see a semi-trailer? Did you know that half the ones you saw were empty?" And that's how he started his pitch,' Chris recalls.

If you don't have a clever anecdote, data can work, too. If you search for Airbnb's pitch deck, this part of their pitch enumerates three problems: travellers are price-conscious, hotels disconnect guests from local culture, and there's no easy way to book a room with a local host. The problem was simple and easy to understand. Best of all, once the investor hears the problem and it resonates with them, they'll be excited to know how the founder intends to solve it.

SIDEBAR: The Birth of the USB Flash Drive

Nowadays, saving files in a universal serial bus (USB) drive is a go-to solution for sharing, storing, or backing up data. But we wouldn't have this ubiquitous tool if it wasn't for a problem that its inventor, Israeli tech innovator and investor Dov Moran, encountered a few decades ago.

It all started in 1998, when Dov was invited to speak at a conference in New York. Just his luck, his computer crashed as he was standing on stage, with 200 pairs of eyes on him. He couldn't push through without the slides because there were exact figures that were crucial to his presentation.

At that time, laptop computers weren't as sophisticated as they are today. And while there were other computers available for use at the venue, there was no way to transfer his file. Luckily, they were able to hook up his computer to a power source to get it just enough juice to do the presentation.

'When I finished my presentation, I took off all the cables and I said to myself, "Never again in my life am I going to come to give a presentation without having a copy in my pocket,"' Dov recalled when I interviewed him for my podcast, *Methods to Greatness*.

Dov experienced a problem and there was no solution available. So, he invented one.

Once he got back to Tel Aviv, Dov worked on his idea. He filed a patent for a USB-based PC flash disk and the rest, as they say, is history.

* * *

People admire Dov for coming up with a solution that took computing convenience to the next level. But out of all the praises and accolades he got for his invention, one particular conversation stands out.

During a flight he took only three months after the USB flash drive was launched, a stranger came up to him and asked if he was the inventor of the tech tool. Dov was proud to confirm.

'He said, "You don't understand it, but I want to thank you because you saved my marriage,"' Dov recalls.

The guy went on to tell Dov that his job was very demanding and that most days, he had to work late at the office. He had two young kids and his wife always complained that he didn't spend enough time with the family.

The USB flash drive allowed him to save his work, go home early for family bonding time, and go back to the computer once the kids were in bed. Everyone was happy—his wife, his kids, his boss.

'When I spoke with this guy whom I'd never met before, I said, "Wow, I didn't know that this is so important,"' Dov tells me. 'I remember, all throughout that flight, I had a smile on my face.

Because, hey, I saved the family life of somebody, and I'm quite happy for that.'

2.   The Solution

If you were playing volleyball, setting the ball is akin to presenting the problem. After the ball has been set into position, it's time to spike it over by offering your solution.

The solution comes from a marriage of two things: first, your perspective of the problem, and second, how you're using your experience, knowledge and skills to solve that problem.

'The pitch is not an act. It is your being,' Anuj Jain, Startup-O co-founder and CEO tells me. 'It's your story of what you're solving, your understanding of the world as it is and how you're changing the world.'

I already mentioned earlier that simplicity is key when it comes to explaining your proposal. But how exactly do you simplify a pitch? Here's a good start: drop the technical jargon. Do away with any word or term that the audience would need to Google.

In addition, take away all the complex parts that would require a listener to attend a three-hour 101 class to understand. As I've mentioned, you'll probably only get five to ten minutes with your audience for your initial pitch. Bombarding them with complicated principles in such a short time would only come off as noise.

Remember what Chris said about the pitch ideally being simple enough that your grandma, who's possibly not very tech savvy, can understand it?

It should also be clear enough that a seventh grader, who likely has limited knowledge and experience in the world, could grasp the idea. Sounds ridiculous? Not really. I've seen it happen on my show.

SIDEBAR: Pitching to a Thirteen-Year-Old

Manila, 2017—FlySpaces founder and CEO Mario Berta straightened his tailored suit and checked his perfectly coiffed hair on the mirror across the hall at the Philippine Stock Exchange. He was waiting for his cue to enter the room where a surprise challenge for *The Final Pitch* was being filmed. I told them they would be pitching their business to a very special panel of investors.

As a young Italian contestant who joined *The Apprentice Spain* some years ago, he knew how to look good and act confident in front of the cameras. His confidence and swagger are unmistakable. You either hated or loved the guy. Besides, he had already pitched to the biggest investors in the Philippines. Whoever the bigwig in that next room was could watch him wing it.

When his turn came, he swung the door open and entered the room.

'Mario, meet our judges for this challenge,' I said while the cameras rolled. His jaw instantly dropped to the floor.

In front of him were four thirteen-year-olds holding play money and waiting for him to pitch.

We conceptualized the challenge with MFT CEO and *The Final Pitch* investor judge, Mica Tan. Mica started investing in the stock market when she was just thirteen years old. For Mica, a startup founder needs to have the ability to simplify their pitch— so much so that it would make sense even to a seventh grader.

Dumbfounded as he was, Mario had to think on his feet. In the simplest way possible, he needed to explain the concept of his digital platform for flexible workspace solutions. He cleared his throat and began to speak.

'When you have your own companies in the future, you will face very big problems. Very greedy landlords who will charge you for a three-year contract for rent,' said Mario, who knew this would get his audience's attention. Any person at any age hates villains—may they be big bad wolves, wicked witches or, okay, greedy landlords.

'This, we're changing today. We'll empower the future generation like you to be able to open big companies that will expand fast,' he added. With that statement, he made the stakes even higher. The judges—the future generation—have become part of the beneficiaries.

He went on to explain his startup in a way he thought was easy to digest. And by the time he finished, the judges were speechless. Mario felt good about himself.

The feeling lasted only for a few seconds until one of the kids said: 'I don't really get your business. How does your business work?'

Yes, Mario totally flubbed the challenge.

* * *

Mario still cracks up about the experience when we talk about it now.

'It was a very uncomfortable and embarrassing moment for me,' he tells me years later. 'I felt completely unprepared because I was ready to start the Mario show and then you completely put me out of my comfort zone.'

Getting out of one's comfort zone surely helps Mario now in his duties as a chairman and director. Plus, it makes for an epic anecdote he tells his business students in Madrid, and in speaking engagements across the globe.

3. The Ask

Now comes the delicate part: the ask, or the call-to-action. What do you want the audience to do after hearing the pitch? Would you want them to be a partner or an investor? Are you inviting them to implement a system you're proposing?

Whatever you're asking, be clear about it. Never automatically assume that your audience already understands what you need just by listening to your pitch. It's normal to feel timid when it comes to the ask. But trying to diffuse the tension by beating around the bush could only jeopardize your pitch by confusing the audience. They, after all, need to know what you're asking for them to decide whether they're willing to give it.

SIDEBAR: A Clear Ask without Room for Misinterpretation

Pitch To Win author and TEDx speech coach David Beckett suggests startups to make the ask so clear, there's a figure attached to it.

'I have one vivid memory of a conversation with an investor who said, "Well, I've seen ten pitches and seven of them didn't say what they wanted, which was really tricky because I'm investing in software companies and we're a ticket size between 500,000 and two million,"' David shares with me.

'My personal opinion is to be direct and put a number on it. If you need €300,000, then tell them so that the people in the audience know if it sits in their range.'

Aside from being direct about your ask, you also need to address another significant factor: what's in it for your audience? Jeffrey Rogers, whom I met at Singularity University in Silicon Valley where he served as our principal facilitator for an executive programme I took, told me about painting a 'preferred future' for the audience during a pitch.

Make the audience the hero of the story so that the pitch isn't all about you or your idea; make the project a collective pursuit and make your audience see that they, too, have a crucial role to play to achieve the project's goal.

In short, don't just drop your ask and hope that the listener says yes. Instead, allow them to appreciate the vision from your perspective and invite them to be part of that future by joining you in the quest.

Elements of the Pitch: The Add-Ons

Apart from the three basic elements, there are other pitch components that you would want to include in your pitch, depending on what you're pitching and where you are in your journey.

For instance, if you're an early-stage startup pitching to potential investors, you may want to show them your minimum viable product, which I'll discuss in the next section. However, if you've been around for a while and have already incurred expenses, revenues, and cash flows, you may need to include your financial projections to show them the potential of your business. Take the time to go over each add-on to gauge if it's something applicable to your pitch.

Here are some optional add-ons to consider based on your situation.

Minimum Viable Product

The minimum viable product, or MVP, is the launchable product with enough features to show your value proposition. The MVP isn't meant to be perfect. Rather, its main goal is to launch quickly and help the team gauge usability and get feedback for further development.

For startup founders, it's vital to create the MVP as soon as possible. During the early stages of a startup, having an MVP shows potential investors that they've tested their assumptions and ideas and that they're getting feedback from their target audience.

I always advise entrepreneurs who pitch on the show to bring their MVP—whether it's a sample of their food or app or invention, nothing beats seeing, feeling, tasting the product. It is also symbolic and tells the other person that you actually have skin in the game and not just basing your ask on a clever amalgamation of ideas and concepts on a slide deck.

The MVP should fit the underserved needs of your target market and there must be enough people willing to use or purchase it because of its value proposition, a concept we call product-market fit. This factor is vital in making a product not only profitable but also sustainable. In fact, StartUp Village co-founder Carlo Calimon says it's often one of the things that investors ask about during pitches, along with valuation, which I tackle in detail in Chapter 7, and the business model.

According to Filbert Richerd Ng Tsai, managing director of the startup-focused consultancy and accounting firm Equity Labs, there are a few ways to show product-market fit. In terms of quantitative metrics, you can use the following:

- **Customer acquisition cost**. This metric applies to almost any startup and pertains to the amount of money you spent to acquire one customer.

- **Cash runway and burn rate**. Applicable for most early-stage companies, cash runway and burn rate go hand-in-hand. Burn rate refers to the rate that an enterprise spends capital to fund overhead expenses before earning positive cash flow. Cash runway, on the other hand, pertains to how long an enterprise can remain afloat before running out of money.

- **Click through rate (CTR)**. A good metric for e-commerce businesses, this shows the ratio of people who see your ad and those who end up clicking it to know more.

- **Average basket value (ABV)**. Also a typical metric used for e-commerce, average basket value refers to the average amount customers spend per transaction.

- **Churn rate**. Typically used for subscription business, this pertains to the rate of subscribers who discontinue their subscription over a time period.

Aside from the quantitative metrics above, you can also illustrate the product-market fit through several qualitative metrics. These include the founders' experience and network, and their prior successful startups. You can also include client feedback as well as customer and employee satisfaction surveys to prove your company's performance.

The Team

If you already have people working alongside you in your initiative or business, you can include who they are in your pitch. By doing so, you're inviting the listener in and allowing them to meet the people behind what's being pitched. According to international law firm founder Doron Latzer, this part needs to be included in the pitch if you're raising money for a startup.

'A prudent entrepreneur, before they get third-party money in, needs to have in my opinion the core team in place,' Doron says. Also, 'It would make a lot of sense if they have an outside advisor or advisory board or somebody from the market or business development who can guide them as to their move forward in the market.'

It always makes sense to have a well-balanced team of founders, each with the experience and skill sets that would complement the others. Ideally, a strong entrepreneur or businessperson can be complemented by someone with a good grasp of the technical aspects or nuances of the business. Having domain expertise or relevant experience in the industry of the problem you are trying to solve is also likely to inspire confidence in the team.

'The team, especially in the early stages, that's what you're banking on,' Katrina Rausa Chan tells me. Kat is the executive director of the IdeaSpace Foundation, the organization behind IdeaSpace Accelerator (the Philippines' longest-running one), and the public-private innovation hub QBO. 'The idea can change, but if you have that kind of team that knows how to run the experiments perfectly, works well together, is driven by a sense of purpose and vision, then you are able to run with that.

Brian Ngan, a venture partner at VU Venture Partners, agrees. Coming from an investor's point of view, he says the founding team can influence his willingness to gamble on a startup.

'A bet in the company is as good as a bet in the founding team,' Brian tells says. 'I want to make sure that our interests are 100 per cent aligned and they have skin in the game.'

Ashley Smithers, a creative extraordinaire who helps companies with their pitches, says the team slide is an integral part of a startup's pitch deck because it shows that you not only have the right product but you also have the right people to pull it off.

She advises startups to not merely throw in a list of names on the presentation. Instead, explain their expertise and experience, and weave that into your company's collective narrative.

Business Model

The business model pertains to the mechanism by which a business aims to generate revenue. To make it simple, this answers the question: how do you make money? Explaining this to your audience will help them understand the business from a deeper perspective and allow them to decide if it's a venture they would want to bet their money on.

'As long as you can build a sustainable business model, you can grow your business,' says Steve Sy, Great Deals E-Commerce Corp. founder and CEO.

It goes without saying that you should know your business model through and through, and it should be crystal clear in your pitch. According to Slidebean CEO Jose 'Caya' Cayasso, you can include the business model in the product section of your presentation to make for a comprehensive narrative that puts the product in the right context.

'The product section, which is everything about the product that can be a combination of product slides, features slides, the business model, and roadmap for future product releases,' Caya says.

While presenting the product alongside the business model, though, make sure that you understand the difference between the two. Speaking from his VC experience, Vynn Capital Managing Director Victor Chua says a lot of founders confuse one for the other.

'The business model is the mechanism, but the tools that you need to get the mechanism to turn is the product,' Victor explains. 'So, there could be companies that have a good business model but the wrong product or the right product but wrong business model.'

For instance, Facebook makes money through advertising. It offers its social networking features for free and earns revenue from users who place ads on the platform. LinkedIn, on the other hand, is anchored on a freemium business model. Creating an account is free, but users need a paid subscription to access premium features.

Institutional investors typically bring in analysts to validate the business model. It's also a significant factor when gauging valuation. According to Equity Labs Managing Director Filbert Richerd Ng Tsai, without the business model, you can't come up with a financial model.

'A lot of the startups say that they're so innovative but at the end of the day, those innovations are really more of an incremental innovation to something that's already existing, so you have to identify which specific industry in the traditional industry you are closest to,' Filbert says. 'As far as valuation is concerned, what is the specific industry you are most closely related to? That will determine the relative valuation.'

To illustrate how the business model influences valuation, Filbert gives the example of a business that offers a water-refilling service through a mobile app.

'You must compare your business model now in two aspects: one, the business model of an e-commerce platform, and two, a business model of a water-refilling station as a retail product,' Filbert explains.

Taking from Filbert's example, you have to determine how much of the business falls under retail and how much falls under e-commerce. Then, you can amalgamate those two factors and present a business model that sufficiently reflects how your business makes money.

Market Analysis

Market analysis refers to the assessment of the market, including its size, the customer segments, and buying patterns. According to Katrina Rausa Chan, your market needs to be big enough but, at the same time, grounded in reality.

'You need to have a realistic understanding of your market and this needs to be big enough but at the same time cannot be so broad,' Kat advises. 'A bad pitch is going to be, like, "to all young people in the country"—it is never true.'

As people in business say, selling to everyone is selling to no one. Telling your audience that you're targeting 'all the young people', would either mean that you're naive or that you don't know your market at all.

Filbert Richerd Ng Tsai chimes in and says it's best to have a specific target market, especially for pre-revenue companies.

'You don't really want too big of a net to capture all the fish because otherwise, you won't be able to afford the net,' Filbert tells me.

Filbert's net and fish analogy makes a lot of sense. To put this into perspective, ask yourself: how much do you have to spend for marketing? Then, do your research on online advertising platforms to find out how much it costs to get your advertisement in front of a certain number of people within your market.

In the end, it all boils down to an achievable market you can afford to acquire. Otherwise, identifying too big of a market can instantly make your pitch seem out of touch and unrealistic.

A crucial part of the market analysis is the competitive analysis. This part discusses who your competitors are in the market and what makes your product unique. Some of the things you may want to compare are the products, market share, and strengths and weaknesses.

For instance, why does your market choose your brand over the others? Do you offer a more affordable solution, or perhaps, better customer service? By pitting your company's analytics against that of other players, your audience can get a bigger picture of your identity, performance, and potential.

Milestones

If the project you're working on has been around for a while by the time you pitch, then it's best to talk about your milestones. Including this in your pitch will allow the audience to see that you're a team that gets things done and that the project is constantly moving and achieving. It also gives investors an idea where you're headed and your stages of growth, and how much resources and funding you will need to get there.

The milestones may include events such as your prototype launch, marketing strategies, key hires, and fundraising history. As it may give investors an idea if you're already earning, you may also want to include your projected break-even point. Remember, though, that this part should be a timeline summary of the major events in the life of the project. You don't have to write a full-on history essay.

A Gantt chart will always do the job in a straightforward manner, but showing the milestones in a simple snaking timeline (there are formats online you can use as references for this) can always give a nice visual peg for your milestone journey.

Financial Projections

Financial projections include a company's expenses, revenues and cash flows for a certain forecast period. This part can be closely tied to your company's valuation, which is the estimate of the company's worth, including its future cash flows.

Mature companies with steady revenues usually value their company using a multiple of earnings before interest, taxes, depreciation, and amortization (EBITDA). For startups, however, this can be a lot trickier and that's why I dedicated a whole chapter to valuation and due diligence alone.

'You should understand your investor math because everything culminates to ask, valuation, equity stake, and so you must be prepared for those basic numbers,' Maria Health co-founder and CEO, Vincent Lau, says.

Bear in mind, though, that many investors won't take your valuation as is. Most of them will question the numbers, and it's up to you to defend them. According to Startup-O co-founder and CEO, Anuj Jain, investors need to challenge assumptions because that's how they gauge if these are well-thought through.

And when it comes to finances, he says: 'There is no substitute for self-learning. You have to be the chef in the kitchen before you can say you run the restaurant.'

The spreadsheet document that shows a company's securities, percentages of ownership, and value of equity is called a capitalization table, or cap table, for short. This is another important pitch element if you've already raised funding previously. According to capital markets lawyer and media tech startup founder Josef Acuña, investors would want to see if they're in good company before deciding if it's a good investment.

'Most investors invest in the people, not really the company,' Josef tells me. 'So they want to see if there's someone who seems like a nutcase on your cap table. Because there are people who are difficult to work with and there are angel investors who might have that reputation.'

Creating the Pitch Deck

A pitch deck is the visual presentation you use alongside your prepared spiel. It could be a PowerPoint presentation, a PDF file or a series of images. Some might presume that the pitch deck is nothing more than an accessory for a pitch. After all, it's the presentation skills and charisma that matters, right? Well, not exactly.

In fact, there are instances when your pitch deck will be sent out there on its own without you explaining each slide. For instance, Cradle Fund Strategy and Venture Development Manager Adam Ramskay says the pitch deck is one of the first things they look at when a startup applies to get into their early-stage programme.

'They go online, they fill out the details, they prepare their pitch deck and they submit everything online. Once our analysts have gone through that, then we'll set a pitching date,' Adam tells me.

Pre-pitch, the slides make for an excellent tool to summarize your idea. The deck somehow acts as a brief so that when you meet your audience, they won't be clueless about what you're presenting.

'The one that's sent to the investor first, a presentation is a living document,' 1821 Design Studio founder Ashley Smithers reminds. 'The presentation that you give to get your invite, it doesn't have you with it. So it should be able to say very clearly what you're doing.'

During an actual presentation, however, the pitch deck should take the backseat. Never ever use it as an idiot board or a teleprompter from which you read your pitch. Doing so will make you look like you don't know your pitch through and through.

'My biggest tip for pitch decks is to not necessarily follow the pitch deck,' Franco Varona, Managing Partner at Foxmont Capital Partners says.

'Decks typically should share stories, not just facts. That's the most important thing. What your deck actually does is ... it is showing that you've learnt something. Taking what you learnt, combining it with your skills, and then pitching the product.'

Franco showed this to me as he whipped out his funding deck for his VC firm Foxmont Capital Ventures. He himself was in the middle of his fundraising round for his $20M fund. His slide on the Philippines' local startup champions, local VCs, and investment growth gave a substantial gist of the country's potential. He ended up using this image as a prompt to then get into a narrative on unlocking international funding in the Philippines.

If you don't have any idea how to craft a pitch deck, perhaps you can take a cue from the most successful ones. Go online and search for the startup pitch decks, such as those of Facebook, Airbnb or Uber. Though some of the versions circulating online are outdated, you can still learn a lot from them.

As for the slide design, it would be best to keep it simple while staying away from passe slide designs of the early 2000s. Hiring a freelance graphic designer would be great, but if you don't have the budget for it, free platforms such as Canva, Crello or Visme will do the job.

But what about the file format for your pitch deck? According to presentation guru Ashley Smithers, you can export your slides to PDF, but it's always best to build it in PowerPoint. Though many users see Keynote as a more intuitive presentation software, PowerPoint is just more widely used.

'Nine times out of ten, if you're sending something to a private equity firm and they want a transaction overview, they're going to want your PowerPoint file,' Ashley says.

Instagram Pitch Deck

Remember the tweet pitch? Well, here's another social media-anchored element you may want to know about: the Instagram pitch deck. This pertains to the multiple-photo posts on the visual social media platform that tell one story or concept.

'Think about a carousel, an Instagram carousel. What is it? It's a slide deck,' award-winning creative Ashley Smithers tells me.

Now, you don't have to upload your whole pitch deck on your IG account. Instead, you'll want to create one multiple-photo post at a time, each explaining an aspect of the business, such as your team, your process, your product, or even trends within your industry.

'That's a huge opportunity. Because somebody would go to your Instagram, and they'll see your pitch deck. They'll see it and they won't even know they've seen it. The detail makes you look put together,' Ashley says.

Having a Go-To Pitch Template

Whether you're making a traditional pitch deck or a version that you're uploading online such as an Instagram pitch deck, it has to show that you know the idea like the back of your hand. When that happens, it doesn't matter how many minutes you're given or if you can present your pitch deck as you speak. And to get to that point, there are two things you need to do: organize and practise.

First, let's talk about organization. During the first phases of getting your pitch together, you probably have a thousand things to say about it. After all, you want your audience to be just as excited about it as you are. However, you need to organize your pitch properly to focus on the key things and take the fluff out.

David Beckett developed a brainstorming tool called The Pitch Canvas©[2] that helps entrepreneurs visualize their whole pitch on

---

[2] You can download a free copy of the Pitch Canvas from David's website, https://best3minutes.com/the-pitch-canvas/, or see a copy of it in the next chapter.

one page. According to David, it's important to map out your content and storyline first before you work on your pitch deck.

'What people tend to do is open up PowerPoint and start typing. But the problem is your brain has a lot of thoughts. It's very random thinking at that stage,' David tells me.

'So what I recommend people to do is take their thoughts out of their head, put them on Post-it notes, get it all out then organize them and then start to build the slight edge to support that story. And then create slides. The tool that is a kind of plug-in for that process is the *Pitch Canvas©*.'

The canvas contains eleven content blocks that will allow you to brainstorm on each specific component. David developed it by talking to people who have listened to hundreds of pitches to find out what they need to hear during the presentation. This is definitely a useful resource if you're having trouble organizing your thoughts and getting your story straight.

Perhaps one of the things this brainstorming tool does is force entrepreneurs to clarify every part of their pitch. How? By forcing them to put it on paper. As a result, they can quickly adjust and assemble an effective pitch depending on the given situation. If, for instance, you're doing a two-minute elevator pitch and only have time to talk about the product and the business model, then you already have a clear idea about what to say.

'A lot of people are very articulate and all, but once you write it down, there are certain expressions that always pop up,' Anuj says. 'There's structure, and you highlight the key phrases. Do a lot of writing, preparation, finding, thinking, and reflecting on how you can convey your message in the most succinct manner. Practise in different settings.'

This leads us to the second task: practise. You don't have to memorize your pitch word by word, but you have to practise it so many times that presenting the idea becomes second nature to you.

Venture fund SOSV General Partner William Bao Bean believes in the adage, practise makes perfect. In fact, he suggests organizing your pitching schedule so that by the time you get to the investors you really want to strike a deal with, you would've perfected your presentation.

'The first time you pitch, it's not gonna be your best. The last time you pitch is gonna be your best,' William says. 'Pitch the people you want money from last, not first . . . By that time, you've answered every question imaginable and you've answered them six times and measured people's reactions multiple times.'

Aside from honing your presentation, pitching to a number of people will also allow you to pick their brains on how to improve what you're building. Let's take the example of Patrick and Alex Gentry's story of pitching to Y Combinator that I recounted at the beginning of this chapter. Though that particular pitch didn't end up in a deal, they were able to get valuable feedback from some of the most experienced startup investors.

'It was something that changed Sprout's trajectory,' Alex tells me. 'Because at that point in time, our clients wanted all sorts of things. It was hard to have the blinders on and say, "No, we're gonna keep on hammering at this problem and be best at it and not worry about all the other potential builds at this point in time."'

The advice that they got from that pitch gave them a new perspective to scale their startup. Now, Sprout Solutions serves more than 1,000 clients by streamlining human resources processes across various industries.

Preparing for Q&A

William Bao Bean is on to something when he talks about practising and answering questions about your pitch over and over. After all, the question-and-answer part that comes after the presentation is perhaps one of the most dreaded portions of pitching.

As a venture capitalist, Amra Naidoo has seen her share of cringe-worthy pitch Q&As. In most of those cases, the founder got prickly when panellists were simply asking questions to understand the pitch better.

'It's the reaction to those clarifying questions that always sours the entire experience. And so I've seen some pretty average or even bad pitches, but they weren't as memorable as the ones who responded really negatively to the questions that were asked,' Amra says. 'I think a lot of them get defensive when people are asking questions.'

Her advice? Don't look at those questions as a threat. Instead, treat them as an opportunity to explain your pitch even further. After all, you're probably given a limited time to pitch and you can use the Q&A to get more 'air time'.

'Sometimes, people are asking questions because they are trying to give you an opportunity to speak more,' Amra says. 'Assume that everyone is coming from a curious perspective and not a mean one. They're not out there to tear you down.'

Aside from embracing a positive attitude during Q&A, making time to prepare for it would certainly help. Earl Valencia, co-founder of Plentina, believes that answering possible questions should be part of preparing for the pitch.

'There's the pregame. Before pitching, think: what are the top five most difficult questions that these people might ask?' Earl tells me. 'If I was that investor, what are the tough questions that I'm gonna ask?'

But it doesn't stop with just knowing the questions. You need to know how to answer those questions. Rather than resenting the queries, see them as a tool to allow your audience to understand your idea in a deeper context.

'The best pitches in my mind are the ones where you are interrupted consistently with questions,' Franco says. 'It's probably annoying, but it gives you the chance to answer the questions in a quick and very smart manner. And more importantly in my mind, it contextualizes the question, it creates a world of stories. And those types of things make an amazing pitch.'

The Long Game of the Pitch

The pitch starts long before the meeting. More than your spiel or pitch deck during the presentation, the pitch also involves who you are as a person—what you've done in the past and what people think of you. In some instances, your reputation may be all there is that lands you a meeting with your audience.

In short, you need to keep a stellar reputation and earn the right to pitch. What have you done in the past and what are you doing right now that makes you worthy of your audience's time? Before meeting you, some people would most likely do a simple background check on LinkedIn or perhaps ask common friends about you. Will they like what they see and hear about you?

In the same way that the pitch starts before the meeting, it also ends long after the meeting. Always follow up.

Roman philosopher Seneca once said, luck is what happens when preparation meets opportunity. There's no telling what happens next when you pitch your idea out there. Will your proposal get approved? Possibly. Will the investor trust you with their money? Hopefully.

But one thing's for sure: not being prepared when the chance presents itself will result in a missed opportunity that may never come again.

'Many people always tell me, "You're always at the right place, at the right time,"' venture partner Brian Ngan says. 'I tell them, "You don't understand how much effort, time and money I put into being in the right place." And then, when the timing comes, chance favours the prepared mind. I just know when to pull the trigger.'

Chapter Assignments

Effective pitching entails organizing your ideas so that it's clear, concise, and easy for the audience to digest. You'll also need to decide which information to include and how to present them to be able to come up with a compact pitch that makes an impact. Here are a few assignments to help you craft and fine-tune your pitch.

- Create a tweet pitch for your idea or business. If you were to encapsulate your idea in 140 characters, how would you phrase it?
- Create a ten-slide pitch deck using an online design platform app. If you were to reduce the slides to five, which ones would you retain?

- From the ten slides you created, list down ten questions an investor would likely ask for each slide.
- Got an idea for a new business or project? Tell people about it. Most often, people are afraid that others will steal their idea or copy it. The value this gives is in getting people's insights, which may help you formulate or expand your thinking even further. Remember that an elevator pitch is not done to close a deal. It is done to open doors.

Chapter 5: Pitching Style and Technique—The Art and Science of the Pitch

In Chapter 4, we delved into the essential pitch elements—The Problem, The Solution, The Ask—as well as some great 'add-ons', so you can have all these down pat come pitch day. You also now hopefully have a better grasp of the different types of pitches you can use depending on your audience, so as to better convey not just the many facets of your startup, but the story behind it as well. After all, who doesn't love a good story—investors included?

In its simplest definition, storytelling is the activity of writing or, well, telling a story. The skill required to tell a story *compellingly*, however, is anything but simple, because it's a skill not everyone is naturally endowed with. In the annals of tech startup history, arguably one of the best is the late Steve Jobs, whose engaging reveals of new Apple products have become tradition for both the company and its highly loyal customers.

But not everyone has the charisma or confidence that Jobs had, especially startup founders who have just started to look into different avenues for fundraising. The inexperienced storyteller need not fret, though, because there is a method to this particular madness; you just have to find one that works for you.

The 'Science' of the Pitch

If you're married, think about the time you and your spouse were still in the getting-to-know-you stage. You probably did your best to look good all the time, to exude the right amount of charm so you could win the other person over. Eventually, you enter into a relationship, and then, once you get to know each other well, make the biggest decision of your lives to get married and build a life together—and the real work begins.

Charm, looks, wit, confidence, maybe a weird sense of humour—the things that may win some people over—may have very little to do with the success and longevity of a marriage. And according to Mohan Belani, co-founder and CEO of Singapore-based startup and tech ecosystem platform e27, it's basically the same when it comes to pitching your startup to investors.

'I think that charisma is always a good starting point to get people interested, and that there's no harm in having good charisma,' Mohan says. 'I think, to a certain level, that can be developed and built, and founders should definitely invest time and effort in that—but they should also be cognizant of the fact that that's not the end-all and be-all [when pitching their startup].'

After all, the best investors can see past the pitch and evaluate whether a company is a good one or not, adds Mohan, whose own venture focuses on helping startups build and grow their businesses.

This is where the science of the pitch comes in, and when I say science, I don't mean formulas and equations, because a business pitch isn't really something you can quantify per se. The 'science' of pitching lies in two key things: preparing your mind, and getting a good grasp of how your audience thinks, too.

It's All in the Brain: Preparing Your Mind

As discussed in the previous chapter, the pitch happens way before you actually face your potential investors or funding sources. Tough questions are to be expected, so the first thing you should do is prep yourself mentally for the task. What US-certified NLP trainer and neurocoach Ben Ampil recommends is to be SELFISH—that is, to Sleep, Exercise, Laugh, and eat Fish—or, basically, to take good care of your physical brain, to ensure that it is in topnotch shape come pitch day.

'Our brain is 2 per cent of our body weight, but it is the most energy-consumptive organ of our body; it consumes 20 per cent of our total caloric intake,' says Ben. 'So imagine you're starting your morning running on coffee, and use your brain to do everything, and your brain requires 20 per cent of what you took—20 per cent of coffee is nothing.'

Exercise is one of the ultimate brain stimulants as it increases your heart rate, which, in turn, pumps more oxygen into your brain. Runner's high is a popularly known phenomenon—that sweet spot where you experience a sense of euphoria as a result of a lengthy run, or an intense form of exercise.

According to an article by the *Scientific American*,[3] research does support the theory that exercise makes you smarter and improves brain function, because physical activity releases hormones that foster the growth of brain cells. Citing research done at the University of California, Los Angeles (UCLA), the growth factors in the brain brought about by exercise enables it to grow new neuronal connections. Another study cited, this one from Stockholm, Sweden, also identifies cell growth caused by exercise as a natural antidepressant.

Israeli entrepreneur and investor Dov Moran, the man behind the invention of the USB flash drive, teaches us a thing or two about keeping his mind and body fit. Aside from sticking to a vegetarian diet, Dov walks 15,000 steps regularly every day. As a rule, he also refrains from taking phone calls while sitting down.

'I'm the walking guy,' says Dov. 'While I talk, I walk—and I walk very fast. If I'm at the office, I walk in the office, and it's the same

---

[3] B. Armstrong,. 'How Exercise Affects Your Brain', 26 December 2018. Retrieved from https://www.scientificamerican.com/article/how-exercise-affects-your-brain/

at home. My target is to not slow down or do worse than before; my target is to do well and to make this world a bit better. That's important.'

Feed Your Brain, Then Organize Your Thoughts

A healthy brain and body is one thing, but to pitch effectively, your mind needs to be organized, too. A billion-dollar startup idea won't mean anything to investors if you can't explain it well to them.

A nifty way to get your thoughts in order was developed by pitch coach David Beckett, and it can be found in one magical piece of paper: The Pitch Canvas, which we also discussed in the previous chapter.

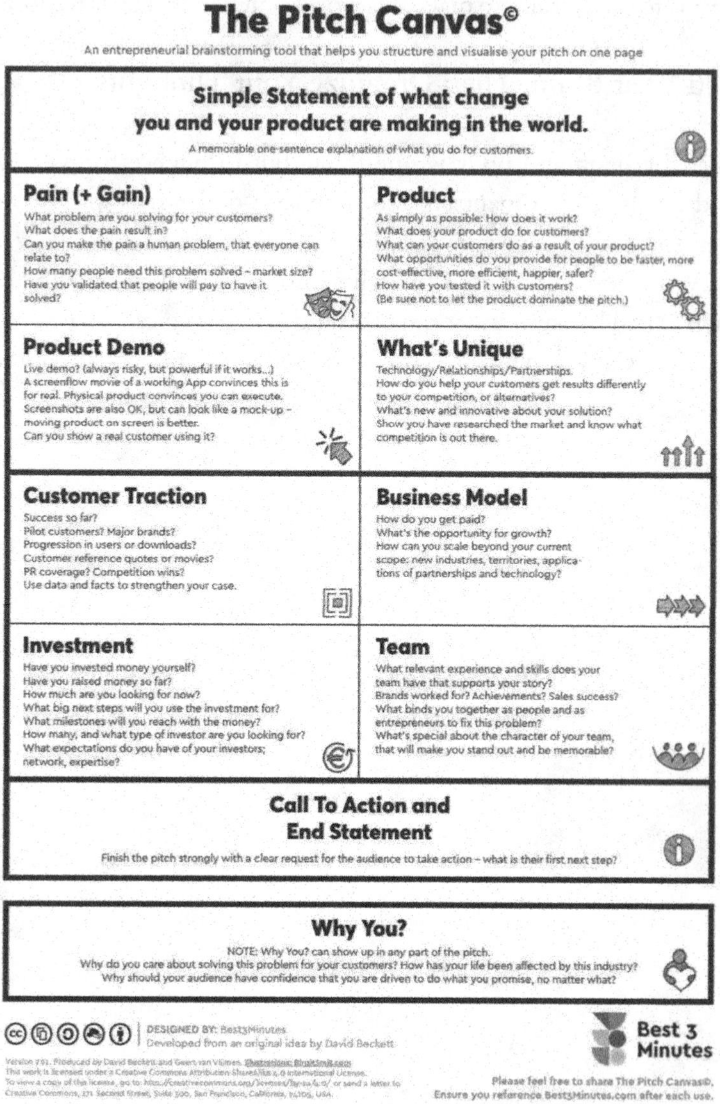
The Pitch Canvas©
An entrepreneurial brainstorming tool that helps you structure and visualise your pitch on one page
Simple Statement of what change you and your product are making in the world.
A memorable one-sentence explanation of what you do for customers.
Pain (+ Gain)
What problem are you solving for your customers?
What does the pain result in?
Can you make the pain a human problem, that everyone can relate to?
How many people need this problem solved – market size?
Have you validated that people will pay to have it solved?
Product
As simply as possible: How does it work?
What does your product do for customers?
What can your customers do as a result of your product?
What opportunities do you provide for people to be faster, more cost-effective, more efficient, happier, safer?
How have you tested it with customers?
(Be sure not to let the product dominate the pitch.)
Product Demo
Live demo? (always risky, but powerful if it works...)
A screenflow movie of a working App convinces this is for real. Physical product convinces you can execute.
Screenshots are also OK, but can look like a mock-up – moving product on screen is better.
Can you show a real customer using it?
What's Unique
Technology/Relationships/Partnerships.
How do you help your customers get results differently to your competition, or alternatives?
What's new and innovative about your solution?
Show you have researched the market and know what competition is out there.
Customer Traction
Success so far?
Pilot customers? Major brands?
Progression in users or downloads?
Customer reference quotes or movies?
PR coverage? Competition wins?
Use data and facts to strengthen your case.
Business Model
How do you get paid?
What's the opportunity for growth?
How can you scale beyond your current scope: new industries, territories, applications of partnerships and technology?
Investment
Have you invested money yourself?
Have you raised money so far?
How much are you looking for now?
What big next steps will you use the investment for?
What milestones will you reach with the money?
How many, and what type of investor are you looking for?
What expectations do you have of your investors; network, expertise?
Team
What relevant experience and skills does your team have that supports your story?
Brands worked for? Achievements? Sales success?
What binds you together as people and as entrepreneurs to fix this problem?
What's special about the character of your team, that will make you stand out and be memorable?
Call To Action and End Statement
Finish the pitch strongly with a clear request for the audience to take action – what is their first next step?
Why You?
NOTE: Why You? can show up in any part of the pitch.
Why do you care about solving this problem for your customers? How has your life been affected by this industry?
Why should your audience have confidence that you are driven to do what you promise, no matter what?
DESIGNED BY: Best3Minutes
Developed from an original idea by David Beckett
Best 3 Minutes
Please feel free to share The Pitch Canvas©.
Ensure you reference Best3Minutes.com after each use.

Fig. 1. The Pitch Canvas, developed by David Beckett

The Canvas, a tool that has enabled David to coach over 1,100 startups and 16,000 professionals through his company Best3Minutes, is divided into blocks that can guide even the most newbie startup founder towards achieving their goal of nailing their most effective pitch.

David says that the Canvas starts simply enough. It asks you how you want to make a difference in the world through your startup, and what that difference is. However, he also says that, much like writing a story, the beginning is almost always the most difficult part.

'What, really, is the problem we want to solve? That's the bit that takes people most time because as soon as they start going through that they suddenly realize that they've been very focused on what they are building,' David says.

Once you overcome that hurdle, David introduces subject 'blocks' that are designed to enable startups to strategically brainstorm about how to present all the different components of their business—be it the product, the traction they've gained so far, or their business model. And then, once you've laid out all the parts, David says the next step is to become selective, because your pitch can't last forever, or even an hour; in fact, he says startups should be able to make their pitch in as short as three minutes. He likens the process to software app development, which requires the developer to not start coding without properly mapping the customer journey of their product's end user.

'Choose the three things that really resonate with your audience, then you start to build that storyline and, effectively, you prototype your pitch,' David says. 'Then make the PowerPoint once you know what you're going to say—and the Pitch Canvas is really the tool that helps the brain.'

Be in the Goldilocks Zone

Another way startups can get their head in the game is to think like a classic fairytale character—Goldilocks. Okay, so she broke into a house that wasn't hers, but the Goldilocks we are referring to here is actually a phenomenon in cognitive psychology and learning called 'The Goldilocks Zone', as described to me by Pascal Finette and Jeffrey

Rogers, co-founder and learning & facilitation principal, respectively, of the be radical Group.

I first met these two brilliant gentlemen when I took an executive programme at Singularity University in Silicon Valley. Jeff was our constant programme facilitator while Pascal was the chair for entrepreneurship and innovation.

They joined forces and founded be radical, an organization that delivers insights to organizations—mainly entrepreneur-led medium- and large-scale businesses—and helps them with their innovation strategy and implementation. They teach their clients to be 'practical futurists'.

The Goldilocks Zone is basically another way that startups can pitch effectively, according to Pascal and Jeffrey, as it enables startups to effectively hook investors by giving them the proper glimpse, and *only* the proper glimpse, of what's in store for them and their investment. Jeffrey says the concept is anchored in what Goldilocks, in the story, looked for as she sampled the three bears' food and furniture—neither too hot nor too cold, neither too big nor too small, and neither too hard and nor too soft, but something *just right*.

'It's a phenomenon in cognitive psychology and learning where you're not overwhelmed, but you also have enough novelty,' explains Jeffrey. 'This is something that has been seen in the cognitive development of infants. When their visual systems are developing, when the brain is starting to develop that capacity, their eyes track to things that are new and interesting but not all really complex.'

For startup founders working on their pitching skills, finding that Goldilocks Zone simply means giving investors the right 'hook' so they take a definite interest in you—what's unique about you?—but not overwhelming them with so much information to the point that they don't see building future business with you.

'It's all about saying, "We're going to be the next big thing. And if you're not investing in us right now, you're likely to lose out,"' says Pascal.

In the same breath, however, Pascal warns us to avoid using fear to encourage investor support. 'Fear is a very bad long-term motivator. It moves you, short-term, but because it drains one's energy, you need to find this interesting balance. Show them that you believe in your work, the work that you're doing will carefully guide a client through a journey, where they will say, holy shit, the future will look different. And then tell the investors: by the way, you're an active participant in this—and here's the future.'

To get into that Zone, just think of the audience—your investors— as the hero of your story, Jeffrey advises. When you make your case, don't just talk about your company's product and your consumers; highlight deeper aspects of your startup, such as company values and culture.

'I think it's important for people to actually understand how they could join you, how they can take part. It's not just about what's coming out of one person's mouth, but it's about how the company is positioned,' Jeffrey says. 'What the company's culture is rumoured to be, how the products are unveiled. You know how every little aspect is curated. So as to create a feel and ultimately I think support a vision of the future and the role that the company plays in making that future real.'

Get in Their Heads

You're in the Zone, and your Pitch Canvas is covered—but even the most organized person will probably get rattled when placed in a room full of people who are all scrutinizing every part of your business. Of course, there's the added tension of you basically asking for them to take a chance on your startup, so, aside from efficiently getting your brain in order, here's another thing you should be mindful of during the pitch: reading the room.

Take it from Mario Berta, who was one of our finalists in Season One of *The Final Pitch*. Like be radical's Pascal Finette and Jeffrey Rogers, Mario is guided by a psychological concept in his pitches: establishing his audience's behavioural baseline.

'You need to be able to detect who that person in front of you is. For me, I gauge the level of Mario that the person in front of me can handle—one, two, three, four, or five?' Mario says, who, at the time of our interview for this book, was definitely delivering at level four or five.

'But if I am in a room with highly successful entrepreneurs who don't speak English very well, I would immediately bring down the level of my speaking pace, the vocabulary I'm using,' he explains. 'And I will most likely use more bullet points and less storytelling, because in storytelling, you need to be able to get your audience to understand the whole story, the whole picture and the humour behind it—jokes, sarcasm.'

To be able to read the room and establish everyone's behavioural baseline in it, one can also make use of icebreakers, Mario adds. His favourite? Watches.

'I'm a watch guy, so 100 per cent of the time if I'm in a room and I see somebody with a nice watch the first thing I say is, "What an amazing timepiece!" The person would, of course, reply with a thank you, and in that sense, I've already conquered the room. These are the small details that you need to be able to identify and use to your advantage,' Mario says.

Reading the room also requires one to pay attention to non-verbal cues, says Ron Baetiong, another *The Final Pitch* alumnus,' who was with us in Season Four where he landed his pre-seed investment for his now thriving startup, Podcast Network Asia. In the ten years that he has been pitching, this serial startup founder and natural sales guy says he has learnt to read a room in just a few minutes.

'In the first two to five minutes, I already know if someone's excited or not. You can read it in their body language. I read it, and I know what to do in just the first two to five minutes,' says Ron. His company, PNA, has enabled Filipino podcasters with a platform for their shows—a company that has now gone regional with its expansion to Indonesia.

While Ron's ability to easily read a room comes with experience, he dishes out a few tips to those who are still getting their feet wet in the startup industry. For starters, while one should pay attention to the audience's body language, he says founders should also be conscious of their own non-verbal cues, because this can also help them gauge if investors are responding to their pitch.

'It's really about creating a body language, the right presentation, the right direction, eye contact—and at the end of the day, looking, sounding, and being credible. You have to give them the right reasons to invest in you. You want to give the impression that, hey, this guy knows what the hell he's talking about. Investors need to go, "I should listen; tell me more,"' says Ron.

It's Not About You

Now, let's backtrack a little here. When we first discussed the science of the pitch, we focused on optimizing our brainpower and organizing our thoughts so that we could get in the Zone, so to speak, and not have our thoughts and ideas all over the place as we present to investors.

However, for a pitch to be effective, you can't just focus on yourself; you have to make your audience feel that the pitch is really about them.

Mario Berta shares more advice on the matter: 'Any kind of sales pitch needs decent preparation, and there are two kinds: empirical, which involves your company, business, positioning, etc., and emphatic, or how to get the person to have an open heart to you.'

If that sounds like dating advice, well, it kind of is; don't you do a little background check on someone you're interested in—like ask other people what kind of food they like, what tickles their fancy?

Think of your investors as someone you'd basically want to go into a partnership with. What kinds of companies do they work with? What about your company would resonate with them?

This ties in perfectly with another important piece of advice from Paula Rizzo, an Emmy Award-winning video and TV producer who is also a media strategist and consultant in the US: don't make the pitch about you.

'This is not about you, the founder; it's about them, so make sure that your message is about them. Why do they care? This is the same thing when you're pitching to the media. Why does the media care? Why does their audience care?' says Paula. 'Of course, you want to get funding, but what is it that they're going to get out of it? Put yourself in their shoes, and then make sure that you highlight that for them.'

Paula, who is also an author, public speaker, and LinkedIn Learning instructor, further advises startup founders to keep key messages to investors short, to the point, concise and clear. As with most people these days, attention spans have become shorter, which gives you a very small window to grab your investors' attention—and keep it.

'If I don't understand your story idea, or I'm not sure what your opinion is, it's just a no, I don't have time for this. I have to go to the next story or the next thing that I'm doing. Same thing with the investors: their time is very precious. So you want to make sure that you can absolutely solidify your pitch, and make sure that you have a condensed version of what it is that you want them to know—and it's about them, it's not about you,' Paula emphasizes.

Earl Valencia, founder of fintech company Plentina, agrees. According to him, making your pitch relatable to your target investors is about fundamentally understanding 'where people are coming from, what got them to their point today, and what drove their success from that point'. So, if you're in front of a CIO, or chief information officer, you'd do well to focus on your startup's technology, and maybe even throw in a reference to how you drew inspiration from a similar piece of tech that that CIO developed some years ago.

That, says Earl, is a sort of pitch science in itself; something he calls 'pattern matching', or the tendency for humans to pattern their behaviour after others to achieve the same kind of success they are aiming for.

'That's why most Asians like to go to good schools: if my nephew went to this good school and he did very well, I would also want my kids to go to that school,' explains Earl, who also in the past, co-founded and led as president the Manila-based incubator and accelerator IdeaSpace Foundation. 'People most likely will do pattern matching, and that's just how I discipline myself mentally. For example, when pitching to a CEO who was an entrepreneur before, you talk about what they did, and your own plans of how to achieve your goals.' Again, he emphasizes for startup founders: do your research first on your potential investors, and get in their heads by organizing your thoughts around these key messages: What is the pain point? How big is this market? Why is it good for them? Why is it good for their customer?

Ben Ampil, motivational speaker and certified NLP practitioner, has another name for this pitching technique—confirmation bias, which we had also touched on earlier in Chapter 3.

'If I am pitching to you,' Ben tells me, 'and you have a similar "playbook", as an entrepreneur, I will sell to you. Because I want you to like me, I would try to watch as many clips of you, watch how you behave. I would calibrate based on your background and level as an investor.'

As final words of advice, Ben stresses that some communication techniques have become 'overused', one of which is neural matching, or what is commonly known as mirroring. When you do this, you basically copy the non-verbal cues, vocal/speech pattern, or attitude of the person you are trying to build rapport with. Ben advises against this technique because it could come off as insincere and over the top.

'The problem with mirroring is that it is so well-known now, that if I did that to you, in your mind you would probably be thinking, "Ben must be crazy; he's imitating me,"' Ben says.

Ultimately, the 'science' of the pitch is all about getting your head in the game in a calculated manner, so as to understand the mindset of your audience. Take time to organize your thoughts, aided by David's Pitch Canvas, and be ready with all the information that will most likely be asked of you come pitch day. It pays to be mentally sharp as well—eating healthy will definitely help you here—so you can 'read the room' more keenly and respond better to your audience.

Do that, and you can start weaving in some art, and heart, to your pitch.

SIDEBAR: The Sciences That Strengthen the Pitch

It has been said that data is today's currency—and for good reason. Companies of all sizes now invest heavily on analysing data, especially consumers', so as to make informed decisions when strategizing on their next business steps. Data analysts and scientists, once unheard of corporate roles, now hold key positions in organizations.

In today's tech-driven startup ecosystem, data is definitely your fuel, especially when making your pitch, says Anuj Jain, who co-founded and is the CEO of accelerator Startup-O, a global startup platform that was built on the premise of bringing fair and equal access for all startups across the world, precisely because he wanted a more scientific approach to the pitch.

'Startup-O comes out of our own journey as a founder, an investor, a scaler, and a mentor—and, more importantly, as somebody who sees the pain and the process of starting a startup and scaling things,' says Anuj, who, prior to joining the startup ecosystem, built an extensive career in the fast-moving consumer goods (FMCG) category, working in large multinational corporations. 'It's not easy, especially in a fragmented geography like Asia, and an evolving ecosystem.'

Anuj and his team discover promising companies, invest in them, and help them scale, weaving the whole value chain of discovery, investing, and scaling using a platform approach. That platform, he explains, is their data science-based technology. 'We have more than 120 global experts from fifteen countries as part of our platform,' he explains. 'Imagine a funnel, every quarter: Startups go through a data science-based screening process, which is less biased, and is geared towards only one thing: Is your product market ready?'

For Jeffrey Seah, a founder's educational foundation also plays a huge part when they are finally facing their investors with their pitch. Anthropology, psychology, and other social sciences will all prove to be useful, according to the Partner for the Asia Fund of top Asian VC Quest Ventures.

'I'm suggesting that because you'll get ideas from anthropologists, psychologists, and maybe a debating expert on how to debate points, how to read people. I think those things help startups,' Jeffrey says.

The Art of the Pitch

Imagine yourself in the business of selling jewellery—not in a fancy, air-conditioned shop, but out on the streets. Aside from peddling to total strangers who would more than likely ignore you or give you the side-eye as they hurry about their day, you have to deal with the exhaustion that comes with being on your feet all day and the fear that someone with less-than-good intentions might try to steal your goods.

This is the exact situation that Ron Baetiong, founder of Podcast Network Asia (PNA), found himself in during one of the Season Four episodes of *The Final Pitch*. Back then, Ron had joined the show to pitch PNA, and as part of his and other participants' journey, they were tasked by one of the investor judges on the show, Tagcash's Mark Vernon, to sell jewellery on the streets of Manila.

As Ron would reveal to me during our interview for this book—a revelation that honestly came as quite the surprise—he devised an unusual way to get ahead of the competition. 'Out of sheer luck, the whole thing was done literally right across my alma mater, the University of Santo Tomas. So we were just peddling around, begging all these students to buy. But as an entrepreneur, you can't do what everybody else is doing: you have to go Blue Ocean,' Ron says, referring to a business strategy wherein one casts a wider entrepreneurial net to explore the untapped market.

'So what I did,' Ron continues, 'and this was not caught on camera: I called my former guidance counsellor. She was literally just stepping out to go home, and I called and said, "Ma'am, come back, I need your help. I will give you your money back, just buy my share." We were behind by a mile, and then she comes and buys 80 per cent of my stash. Then after the taping, I went to her and gave back her money.'

This reminds me of Spanx founder Sarah Blakely, who in a Lewis Howes podcast I listened to tells the story about landing her first retail deal with American department store Neiman Marcus and asking her friends to fake-buy her Spanx undergarments from the seven stores they placed them in so she can create the buzz. There was a lot of hustle involved, and she personally stood in the store and talked about the product from nine to five, explaining to people what her invention can do for women's bodies.

Going back to Ron, what he points out in this story is the value of using your unfair advantage to give yourself an edge over your competition—something which would definitely come in handy when you are pitching to investors alongside other startups.

At the end of the day, you need to look at your unfair advantage all the time,' Ron says. 'My unfair advantage was that I was at my freakin' alma mater—so what do I have? A *network* in my freakin' alma mater.'

Knowing your unfair advantage or your edge, among other things, when crafting your pitch now heavily comes into play as we leave the realm of reason and dive into the rhyme, the art of the pitch. Unlike science, the art part is more subjective; it's all about how you present yourself, how you speak, how you tell your story, how you grab and retain audience interest throughout your entire speech, and even how you look.

In short, how creative can you get with your pitch to get your story across—and make it compelling enough to get you to your ultimate goal of winning over your audience?

Unleash the Storyteller in You

When we opened this chapter, we talked about the importance of compelling storytelling in pitching, and how being methodical about it can greatly help us organize what we want to talk about. But, as with any story, the audience reading about or listening to and watching it will always look for a hero to cheer for.

Just think of the most well-loved movies known around the world—*Star Wars*, *Harry Potter* the Marvel Cinematic Universe—these epic stories, heroes, and characters are the stuff that world-renowned literature and film empires are made of. However, great storytelling isn't just confined to the creative industries.

In the startup ecosystem, the pitch is an entrepreneurs' main storytelling tool. It would help, however, to stretch our minds a bit to take a page from the entertainment industry, specifically, a particular storytelling genre: reality TV. It may not be obvious, but there's a lot to learn from how these reality shows have successfully captivated the minds and hearts of millions and catapulted people and even brands to worldwide fame and success.

In my opinion, producer Mark Burnett is one of the most effective storytelling entrepreneurs in recent times. The man has successfully built a media empire around the reality TV genre, which he effectively introduced into the mainstream at the turn of the millennium. When Burnett's social experiment *Survivor* first entered public consciousness in May 2000, the premise was too controversial to resist: sixteen castaways marooned on a deserted island where they needed to 'outwit, outplay, and outlast' each other.

He is a master of pitching the premise of a TV show concept to network executives and the stars of these franchise reality shows— Sylvester Stallone and Sugar Ray Leonard for *The Contender*, the recording artist judges of *The Voice*, and, of course, Donald Trump for *The Apprentice*.

For what it's worth, many are of the opinion that Burnett was largely responsible for mythologizing Donald Trump as an icon of American success and paving the way for his rise to the presidency. In an article in *The New Yorker*, Katherine Walker, a producer on the first five seasons of *The Apprentice* said, 'I don't think any of us could have known what this would become. But Donald would not be President had it not been for that show.' The anathema of *The Apprentice* is that it allowed Trump the opportunity to resurrect his image and craft his own narrative as a powerful, successful, no-nonsense capitalist, but we all know how that went—Trump went on to become the most divisive president the United States has ever seen.[4]

---

[4] P. Keere, "How Mark Burnett Resurrected Donald Trump as an Icon of American Success," *The New Yorker*.
https://www.newyorker.com/magazine/2019/01/07/how-mark-burnett-resurrected-donald-trump-as-an-icon-of-american-success

On the other end of the spectrum, we have *Shark Tank*, one of the most successful TV shows created in terms of positively impacting America's already entrepreneurial mindset. Burnett, through Kevin O'Leary, Mark Cuban, Lori Greiner, Barbara Corcoran, Robert Herjavek, and Daymond John, were able to put entrepreneurs and business ideas into primetime TV, launching the businesses of these entrepreneurs and inspiring millions to take their own entrepreneurial journeys.

So what binds all these great storytelling ideas and formats together? According to Burnett, they all echo the established storyteller patterns of *The Hero's Journey*.

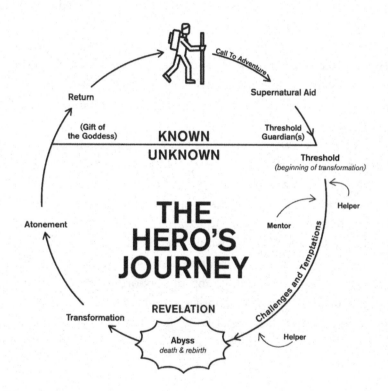

The Hero's Journey

The Hero's Journey is a mythic structure developed by the late American author Joseph Campbell, who wrote *The Hero with a Thousand Faces*, and is most known for his work on comparative mythology. Now a common narrative archetype, The Hero's Journey has been extensively cited and talked about by the likes of Mark Burnett, Silicon Valley execs, and thought leaders all over the world. It has twelve stages:

- Ordinary World. The start of the story, where we see the hero in his pre-adventure state. Here, the storyteller presents the hero's characteristics that audiences can relate to.

- Call to Adventure. Here, the hero faces a turning point—a challenge, a threat—and he or she has to decide whether or not he or she will embark on the journey to resolve the issue.

- Refusal of the Call. Of course, a hero will naturally have doubts and fears, which would make him or her backtrack a bit or even refuse to rise up to the challenge—which would result in serious consequences.

- Meeting the Mentor. Behold! The hero meets his or her mentor, and through that mentor's guidance, overcomes his or her fears, and starts again on his or her quest.

- Crossing the Threshold. This is the moment when the hero jumps into the unknown, leaving the familiarity—and safety—of his environment.

- Tests, Allies, Enemies. What's a quest without these three? At this stage, the hero needs to be able to look out for himself and gauge who is out to get him, and who his friends are.

- Approach to the Inmost Cave. This is the calm before the storm, where the hero takes a pause as he enters the belly of the beast. All the doubts and fears resurface ... but this time, despite those, the hero is ready to face his main challenge.

- Ordeal. The main event, where the hero goes head-to-head with his or her personal challenge.

- Reward (Seizing the Sword). Our victorious hero emerges, having defeated his enemy and survived death—and even takes with him a reward.

- The Road Back. This stage is much like the Call to Adventure, but now, the hero may face a choice between returning home or facing a greater enemy for a higher cause.

11.   Resurrection. This is usually the climax of the story, wherein the hero defeats the ultimate enemy, and is 'reborn' after succeeding.

12.   Return with the Elixir. The hero is back to where he or she started—and is a changed person.

While that might have read like the stuff of fantasy or science fiction, The Hero's Journey could be a useful tool when crafting your pitch. You could paint yourself, or even your customer, as the hero, and from there, weave in the narrative of your startup, without forgetting all the important elements. We discussed David Beckett's Pitch Canvas earlier, the parts of which you can bake in your hero story; on top of that, David advises startup founders to keep in mind that pitching is basically public speaking, which can make the task all the more daunting.

But does the hero get intimidated? Yes, perhaps—but that doesn't mean he or she quits. As a pitch coach, David's style is to 'break down' startup founders so they can build themselves back up again. And whether it's through David's Pitch Canvas, or the hero's journey, or a clever combination of both, breaking down your startup story through a narrative approach can make for quite the compelling case. Perhaps you started as an underdog, with a startup idea that has received multiple rejections, until you found the right partner? Or was establishing a startup your response to that Call to Adventure?

Our show *The Final Pitch* is, essentially, the Hero's Journey of entrepreneurs. They are called to adventure, meet mentors, go through challenges, seize the investment, and return a changed person. Within the show you'll also find the respective hero's journeys of the investor judges, and zooming out, my personal hero's journey as the show's creator and host. Multiple narratives, told at different times, but following the same story arc.

Weaving the personal with the professional, according to Millennial Influencer and Marketing Strategist Chelsea Krost, is also part and parcel of storytelling during a pitch. It introduces your investors to your personal brand, which should be in line with your company's. 'Your story—your brand—is a combination of the experience you've lived, the lived life that has brought you to this point today that has shaped you for this moment, that has given you the reason, the cause to create what you're pitching,' says Chelsea, who, at thirty, is an accomplished speaker, author, TV and radio talk-show host, a LinkedIn instructor, and a proud new mom.

'You are the solution. You or your product is going to solve my problem. The way you share your solution is storytelling. It's really how you're weaving your story into your pitch that's going to make the investor get to know you, get to understand why you're passionate for this cause, get to know why you're the person to drive it to the finish line. And it's going to be the reason they believe in you, to get it done right,' she adds.

Using the Hero's Journey isn't required, of course, to create a winning pitch. But if you believe it can help you connect better to your potential audience, it won't hurt to heed the Call to Adventure.

Mastering Conversation

Now, there are many times when storytelling doesn't happen on a stage or in an organized pitching event or meeting. Sometimes, as Anuj Jain, co-founder and CEO of Startup-O, a global venture platform for startup assessments, investments and business scaling, says: A pitch can happen, and succeed, in the middle of a house party, while you're chatting over a glass of wine, without the pressure of being onstage with all eyes on you. Intimate conversations are more casual and relaxed, which is great, but it could also be tricky talking shop when your targeted investor isn't in the right environment to receive a sales pitch.

While I can't prescribe exactly how to master the art of creating good conversation, we can learn from some startup founders who've been successful with their own signature style. Ron Baetiong, for example, uses humour, because comedy comes natural to him.

'I try to infuse my personality, and my objective in those first two minutes is to make you like me. The way I do that is to make you laugh, because you can now associate me with something positive,' says Ron. 'If I don't make you laugh, that means there's no connection between us. Whatever I say is bullshit to you after, and I don't want that to happen.'

Amra Naidoo, co-founder of award-winning startup accelerator Accelerating Asia and general partner at Accelerating Asia Ventures, says that infusing your pitch with a bit of 'flair'—your personality, your energy—wouldn't hurt, especially when engaging someone in conversation. 'And I can't remember who it was that said people will never remember what you said, they only remember how you made them feel,' Amra adds. 'So, at the end of the day, yes, get your main concept out there; but people feel your energy, they feel your life and your passion for whatever you're doing. So, I think that's more important than the exact words.'

The energy that startup founder and investor Jacqueline van den Ende brings to casual conversations with investors is one that isn't just confident, but also smooth and cool. 'Don't come off as someone who is asking for money,' she advises. 'Talk to investors about all the other people that want to invest in you and those who are onboard, and if they see your potential, they will be the one to offer you the investment.'

Whether suave, humorous or dramatic, it's important that you feel confident in your skin when you are speaking, advises Ashley Smithers. Find a style that fits you, and don't try to be like somebody else. 'Not everyone can be like Steve Jobs,' she tells me. 'You can see it, when someone is confident about their pitch. You can see how their body language changes and how they talk faster.'

Ron pretty much has the same tip. For him, his comedic timing works because he enjoys making people laugh. He acknowledges the fact though that not everyone can be funny, and that comedy is something that is pretty hard to teach.

'Stay true to yourself; don't be a comedian if you're not,' says Ron. 'In the end, you also need to make sure that you are credible.'

Looking the Part

I distinctly remember this one entrepreneur I personally invited to pitch on our show. She was brilliant, an AI expert, and clearly knew her stuff.

You could tell she was an engineer, and exuded this devil-may-care look that, quite frankly, made her look like she really didn't care about how she looked. When she talked about her startup, she had a nervous energy that made her fascinating to listen to. She also had a slight lisp that added to her mad scientist eccentricity. I got to talk to her quite casually, and we were able to strike up a good conversation on why she was doing what she was doing and her goals for her company's future. In my mind I was thinking, 'If our investor judges can get past the raw packaging, there is a real gem here.'

Fast forward to her initial pitch on the show. True to unkempt form, she looked like she had just gotten out of bed. It may have been her high ask, but a part of me secretly wished it was not her physical appearance and lack of polish that prevented her from getting picked by the investor judges to move to the next round. Still, if you're asking for millions of pesos in funding, the least you can do is show a little effort and comb your hair.

Venture capitalist Jeffrey Seah agrees. 'Gone are the days when you see startup founders that are geeks with pimples and hair that's messy, wearing a white t-shirt. Today, we don't see such founders. Today, founders come very coiffed, good-looking, well-packaged, with beautiful PowerPoints: they're a real view.'

For *The Final Pitch*, we always advise our entrepreneur contestants to dress corporate casual—that's a blazer for men, and a dressy blouse for women.

'I'm Italian, so, for us, fashion is important, of course. You can only gain points by looking good,' says Mario Berta.

However, Mario also clarifies that 'looking the part' of a startup founder doesn't stop at the clothes you choose to don. The confidence you wear also adds to your entire branding, and it should be a confidence that is elegant, not arrogant, Mario says. And confidence doesn't equate to perfection, either; Jeffrey Seah says founders shouldn't hide their flaws, and be as authentic as they can be when pitching, especially these days when one can create a whole different persona on social media.

'I want to see authentic and genuine. I have seen startups that had to learn to be authentic. Authenticity is very important; in the startup world, the VCs are giving you real money, and they want to know where their money is going,' says Jeffrey. 'Startup founders shouldn't be pressured to hide flaws, like speaking with a lisp; instead, they can show their shortcomings and transform them to become strengths. The flaws then become their differentiating factor.'

Are You Camera-ready? Pitching in a Post-Pandemic World

Up until last year, entrepreneurs pitching their businesses did so largely in physical events, face-to-face with their audience. By now, we know that the coronavirus disease has changed the way we do a lot of things, pitching included; and with lockdowns happening left and right, everyone has adapted and learnt how to keep the world running without leaving the four corners of home.

In *The Final Pitch*, for instance, we had to hold our Season Six press launch virtually through Zoom and broadcast it through Facebook live. The next season, we went hybrid and had the contestants pitch to a virtual investor panel strewn across the city in their respective offices and homes. Just like us, many other entities across various industries turned to online resources to get the work done.

Life must go on. Cogs must keep turning, especially those in the startup ecosystem.

Pre-Covid, founders didn't need to worry too much about looking good on video. Unless, of course, they're pitching on a reality show like *The Final Pitch*. As its showrunner, I've seen my fair share of contestants crumbling under the combined pressures of convincing the investors to say yes while trying not to look awkward on camera. It never gets easy.

In the new normal, pitching through a recorded video or doing it live through a video conference has become an accepted practice. This means that aside from mastering your pitch, you'll also need to learn the technicals and present yourself well as you make 'eye contact' with that tiny black dot that is your webcam.

How We Watch Videos

Before we discuss how to create a good pitch video, let's first tackle how people these days, including your audience, typically watch videos. According to Quest Ventures partner Jeffrey Seah, who also has an extensive background in advertising, vertical storytelling has become a popular technique with the dawn of video-sharing and streaming apps.

'Everyone is using their thumb to move, and it encourages vertical action,' Jeffrey explains. 'People used to look at things from left to right, there's no up-down. But how do you stop people from scrolling? The day you can stop them from scrolling, that's the new primetime.'

The main takeaway here is that our attention span has become even shorter over the past decade, and that includes the time we spend on each video we view. We can now control everything with a tap of a thumb. And with new media platforms anchored on instant gratification, we've developed an urge to click 'skip ads' on YouTube or 'play something else' on Netflix if we don't like what we're seeing.

'You need to capture attention right from the very beginning. You need to be engaging,' former senior TV producer Paula Rizzo advises.

If you don't want your audience to zone out during your video pitch, or worse, close the video file before you even get to the heart of your pitch, you need to make it worth their time.

How to Create a Pitch Video

Taking out your camera phone and pressing the record button is easy. But how do you create a video that your audience will actually want to watch? TEDx speech coach and author David Beckett says it doesn't have to be too elaborate.

'You've got the choice to just talk to the camera or talk over the slides. My recommendation is a combination of both, nothing too fancy, but they need to see you,' David advises. 'They need to see the content and the slides help them understand the story.'

There's a wide variety of apps that will allow you to record your screen, webcam, and audio all at the same time. As for the technical setup, it would be the same as when you're pitching live via video conference.

Here's a quick rundown of the technical stuff you'll need to get in order before you record your pitch or get on a video conference call:

- **Computer or laptop**. Make sure that your device is in proper working order. If you're recording a video, tinker with the app or platform ahead of time before your actual 'taping' schedule. If you're live pitching, and you'll be using a video conferencing app you've never used before, practise the call a few days before to catch any issues or settings you may need to adjust. To do so, you can start a video call alone or call a friend to test your device. There is absolutely no excuse to be late for a video conference call, and sometimes failing to log in can be what does that. Make sure that your device is fully charged, or better yet, plugged to an electric outlet.

- **Webcam**. In broadcast, we have what we call an eye-level shot, used for news reports and interviews. To achieve this, the camera is placed at a height the same level as the eyes so that the subject is looking straight at the camera without tilting the head up or down. This is also the best way to present yourself during a video meeting. If you're using a laptop, use a stand or perch it on top of a stack of books so that the camera is about the same level as your eyes.

- **Audio.** Whether you're using a headset or your laptop's internal mic, ensure that your voice comes through clearly without any distracting echoes. Record an audio file to check how you'll sound. If you're pitching live on a video conference, make sure that your speaker system is working well so that you'll be able to hear any questions or comments clearly. If there is danger of extraneous noise interrupting the call (construction works or the sound of a crying baby), move to another location.

- **Lighting**. Being in a room that's well-lit or that has an ample natural light source, such as a window, is usually enough. However, if the place where you're taking the video call is too dark, you can use a ring light to illuminate your face. You can also use a desk lamp if that's what you've got at home, but don't point it directly at your face. Instead, point it to a wall behind the laptop to diffuse the light, providing a more natural effect. During daytime, don't position yourself with your back against an open window. Doing so will create a silhouette effect, and you'll risk looking like an anonymous whistle-blower being interviewed on TV.

- **Background**. A clean, professional background will suffice for formal meetings. If you can't find a good-enough spot in your home, you can simply blur or change the background through the video conference app. Some people go the extra mile of using a customized background graphic with their logo in it. This surely makes one look more professional, but it's completely optional. The neatness or messiness of our background is also indicative of our respect to the people we're talking to. If you don't mind the other person seeing an unkempt bed or a collection of random unsightly artefacts that distract your pitch, you've got a problem.

- **Internet connection**. This one is especially crucial for live pitches. Make sure you have a stable internet connection on the day of your video conference. When you're pulling out all the stops to present yourself and your idea the best way you can, the last thing you need is a choppy connection that will garble your audio, freeze your video, and flush all your efforts down the drain. If you're sharing your internet bandwidth with other people, request for you to have sole access during your call. Bribe everyone if you have to.

- **Don't be the BBC Man**. The viral interview of Professor Robert Kelly on BBC where his toddler and wife interrupted his interview was hilarious and downright adorable at the time, but working from home is no longer an excuse not to keep distractions at bay. Lock the door.

The good thing about a recorded video is that it allows you to pick your best take and even possibly improve your presentation with simple editing before sending it to the recipient. But being given the chance to pitch on a live call is always better.

How to Nail a Video Call: Advice from Two Emmy Awardees

Though pitching via video conference may seem easy (you can, after all, do it while wearing pajamas and no one will be the wiser), making an impact can be more challenging when there are so many distractions between you and your audience.

Think about this for a minute: how many times have you attended an online meeting and secretly browsed your social media feed or email while absent-mindedly nodding in agreement to the presenter? It might be safe to say that, at one point or another, we've all been there. In addition to that, your audience may possibly have more distractions at home or in their office, making it difficult to catch their interest compared to if you were meeting them face-to-face in a closed conference room.

As I write this book, I was fortunate enough to get in touch with two Emmy award-winning communicators who generously shared their knowledge on how to present effectively even through a video call.

In my podcast, Methods to Greatness, I've had the pleasure of interviewing Jessica Chen, a former news reporter for ABC ten News who won an Emmy in 2017 for her coverage of the San Diego wildfires. Soulcast Media, the strategic business communications agency she founded, helps Fortune 500 companies and entrepreneurs hone their communication skills and executive presence.

As part of my research for this book, I also interviewed Paula Rizzo, a media strategist and former senior TV producer who, coincidentally, also won an Emmy during her days at Fox New Channel in New York City. She trains executives and personalities on being camera-ready for media appearances and helps clients with media pitching and video series development.

Here are valuable tips on online presentation from my conversations with these two communication experts.

Tip 1: Put effort into your video calls.

Jessica Chen (JC): Don't underestimate how important the way that you carry yourself is, the way that you're speaking on camera. Impressions are always being made. Even though you work with your team for many many years, trust me, they're still looking, what kind of background is going on, what it is you're wearing. So, putting in just a little bit of effort can really help.

Paula Rizzo (PR): Lots of people are now doing virtual meetings to pitch, and it comes with a bit of a different mindset. It's not innate and native for everyone to look at the camera and treat it like a person, but it's something that you should be practising every single day when you're on a video call ... If you have to, take a picture of the person that you're looking to pitch to right there on your screen so you can visualize and think about who it is that you're looking to connect with— that's very important.

Tip 2: Work the Camera.

JC: You might have seen people get on Zoom calls, and the camera is looking up their nose. Or they're so close to the camera that it is not the most comfortable viewing experience for the person on the other side. I say, [putting] little bits of effort into how you carry yourself makes a huge difference.

PR: Connect with the camera. Look at the camera as if it's a person, and don't be looking down at the people so you'd be able to see them on your screen. Instead, really connect and look into the camera because for the person who's viewing it, they feel like you're looking at them. You're asking them to fund you or to back your company or whatever it is that you're asking them for, so really talk to them genuinely ... Connect with a person.

Tip 3: Pay attention to body language and voice quality.

JC: Communication is what you say, your body language, and your tone. People only think it's usually the first one, but really, it's the marriage between these three. So when I communicate, especially on video, since there's a barrier, there's a distance between you and me, I try to make sure that I am incorporating body language as much as I can, I'm using a variety of my voice, because that's how you build engagement.

PR: One thing that I tell people to do is to fill the room with the sound of your voice. I'm the only person in the room right now, but I am presenting to this camera, and so I make sure that it comes across like I'm passionate—which I am—about what I'm talking about. The way to do that is to fill the room with a full, clear voice, and that you're able to get across what you know powerfully and connect with the person on the other side of the screen.

Tip 4: It's all about the energy you project.

JC: When it comes to presenting your idea, pitching your idea, I say your energy level on camera is so important. You have to be mindful of your energy and how you're showing up, which goes into the tone of voice. A lot of people when they speak, they can speak in a very monotone voice, and that's just not very interesting for people to listen to and that's a fact. So when we talk about variety, it's talking about speeding up, slowing down, going high, going low, and choosing the words you would want to emphasize, and when you get to that word and when you hit that word, then you slow down.

PR: You have to up your game when it comes to video. When you're not in the same room with someone, you have to pretend that you are, and one of the ways to do that is to really make sure that your excitement level and your energy are up. You don't want to just be monotone, you want to make sure that you are connecting in a very powerful way.

Lastly, a pro tip from Paula when pitching via video calls: speak in soundbites. She calls this the Accordion Method, which she teaches as part of a media training lesson for her clients.

'My background is as a TV producer, so my ear is trained to hear and listen for soundbites—but not everybody thinks and listens that way. The Accordion Method is all about finding a short, medium, and long way to talk about anything that you're going to talk about,' Paula explains. 'In that short headline that you're giving people, they should be able to take away great value and know what it is that you want them to know right off the bat. So after that, if they zone out or you get interrupted or whatever it is, you know that they've gotten value out of what you've said.'

Pitching virtually requires a bit more effort if you want to do it right. After all, the delivery, tone, and manner by which you conduct yourself are equally as important as your message.

Though you'll need to exert extra effort in technical preparations, this avenue surely paves the way for a whole new world of possibilities for you and your business. Though virtual pitches have allowed us the convenience to never make geography a restriction, it should also make us never take for granted our ability to put our best foot forward.

The Pitch Deck: Tips and Tricks

Outside of the elevator pitch or pitches that happen in a business mixer, the deck is pretty much a staple tool for startups. As described by Ashley Smithers, principal at 1821 Design Studio, whom we first met in the previous chapter, the deck is 'the movie that you're forming in somebody's head that you want them to talk about' after the pitch.

And in today's environment, with meetings mostly happening virtually, the pitch deck has become even more important for startups to convey their data and solution more clearly, says Kalibrr's Paul Rivera.

When it comes to what should go into your pitch deck, arguably the most popular method is Guy Kawasaki's, which prescribes that one can condense all the info they want to present to simply ten slides, present for no longer than twenty minutes, and use a font size that's no smaller than thirty. For this book, however, I've decided to gather multiple insights from startup founders, investors, and design experts such as Ashley, to serve not as the ultimate rule for creating pitch decks, but to help you craft the presentation that works for you and your company.

Deck Design

Design is important in the sense that anything that is visually appealing will likely grab the attention of your audience. Pictures, as the adage goes, say a thousand words, and Ashley emphasizes how essential it is to use the right images to complement your pitch.

'The use of imagery and the use of presentation is really essential to getting your business model across. It should not be just a chart saying this is how we operate; it should be a chart that says, this is how we're going to affect lives,' Ashley explains. Deck design can also focus on and play up your branding, which means consistency in the elements you use—the shapes, the colours—is required throughout your slides.

Ultimately, visuals should serve a precise purpose if they are to make it on your deck. Moreover, Paula Rizzo highlights the importance of your deck supplementing your pitch, and not overpowering you and what you're saying.

'I love using visuals, but I find that people overuse slide decks and they hide behind them, especially when we're talking about video. So if you're doing a presentation, I want to make sure that you are full screen first when you're introducing, and you're talking about who you are, so that you can truly connect with the other person on the camera on the other side of that video call,' Paula says. 'You should be using graphics and videos only to supplement what it is that you're talking about. Is there a pie chart that I can show that will really illustrate this point that I'm talking about? How can we show growth in the next ten years? Something like that.'

Victor Chua, founding and managing partner at Southeast Asia-based VC Vynn Capital, also reminds startup founders that VCs appreciate good deck design—i.e., the simpler, the better.

'The decks that I like the most are the simplest. We don't need fancy design or a lot of animation. As long as it helps me identify the stuff I want—what are you doing, what problems are you solving, how much can you make, who are you and your complete advantage—then it works. That might sound too straightforward, but VCs don't always have a lot of time to spare,' says Victor.

Content is King

Jose Cayasso, more popularly known as Caya, founder of Slidebean, uttered these words above during our interview with the side comment, 'My team might kill me for saying this,' he says, chuckling; after all, his company promises startups the ability to 'raise millions with awesome pitch decks'. But he makes it clear that, yes, content takes precedence, and design's role is to complement the information that you put in your deck.

'I've seen badly designed decks raise funding, as long as the content is good. I've never seen bad content with good design raise funding. So content will always prevail in this matter, and that's something our company has been committed to, as we care about helping startups,' says Caya, who has also spoken at numerous tech and startup conferences, one of which is TEDx.

You might wonder—does this mean an awesome deck design wouldn't matter at all during a pitch?

Not exactly, says Caya, because great aesthetics still speak volumes about a startup founder's eye for design—which would be a reflection of how well you can package your product.

But, as Victor pointed out, there is certain information that investors would want to see right away when you present, and they don't always have the time to read through your deck. So what should be in your deck?

According to Caya, these are the sections you need:

- The Intro. Basics about you, your company.
- The Status Quo. This talks about the business opportunity you've seen based on what's happening in the world now.

- Product. This part should be all about what you offer and your target market.
- Market. Expound here about how you are reaching your target market, how you are penetrating it, and why this is relevant to your investors (i.e., how much are they going to make from this?).
- Why Us? In this section, allow yourself to brag about your competitive advantage as a company, and why your startup is in the best position to solve the problem you are solving.
- Asset. Here, you can dive into how much you would need to continue building your company.

Ashley Smithers says she also likes to include a 'meet the team' slide, as we discussed in the previous chapter, just to showcase that you don't have just the right product in place, but the right people, too. She also dishes this piece of advice: 'Do one idea per slide and make it simple and clear. What you're saying matters more than the beauty of the slide. The slides need to have bones without decoration. Look at the presentation in a black and white scenario without anything else, so that if something breaks down, the message and content are still speaking for you.'

As a best practice, founder of Netherlands-based Carbon Equity Jacqueline Van den Ende, likes to send a copy of her pitch deck in advance to the investors she is meeting, together with a voiceover of her presentation. She does this so that during her virtual pitch, her audience looks at her and hears her message instead of staring at her slides. 'Never on Zoom do you want to go through a pitch deck with investors. That doesn't work; you want to be looking at each other, not at slides, and what I'm trying to do is to compress the story of Carbon Equity into a one- or two-minute pitch: what is the core of what we're doing, the problem we're solving, what's the size of opportunity, who else is addressing that opportunity, and why are we the best team to make that happen. And then we dive into the questions. So that one-, two-minute pitch is very important to get the key points that are critical to get your message across,' says Jacqueline, who has gone full circle in her startup journey, having been both a founder and investor.

What Jacqueline describes is akin to what Caya calls the Email Deck, which he says is one of three types of pitch decks, the other two being the Demo Day Pitch Deck and the Meeting Deck. These three differ based on the context of their use.

For one, Caya says most startup presentations are meant to be emailed, because when you meet an investor, chances are they will ask you to send a document containing the information they need to get to know your business more. The Email Deck, therefore, needs to be created in such a way that investors won't spend more than four minutes reading a slide, because, according to Caya, anything that takes longer than that to digest won't stick to a person's mind.

'If you need more than four minutes to digest the information, you're going to lose people along the way. We've tracked this activity, and my approach to the four-minute timeframe comes from real data. The number of slides doesn't matter, as long as you stay within that time frame,' Caya says.

The Email Deck and Meeting Deck, he adds, can be very similar; however, with the Meeting Deck, the four-minute reading time frame doesn't need to be strictly adhered to, since an arranged meeting with investors gives startups more time to do a deep dive into what they do, what they offer, and all other details about the business model.

As for the Demo Day Pitch Deck, or the regular ten- to fifteen-slide deck that gives a general introduction to your company, this can be more visual, since the assumption is that the founder is there to talk through the slides.

The Devil is in the Details

Focused, consistent, and fundable—this is how you present yourself to investors when your pitch deck is flawless, says Ashley Smithers, so make sure you pay attention to every detail that you put into your presentation. She says it's great to make your design as beautiful and streamlined as you want it to be; but for every visually striking slide with one bold image with hardly any text or data, make sure to back that up with three more that are 'decently gridded' and actually have the information your investors need presented in a way that would still be easy to grasp.

'I don't want to see data in sentences, I want to see data pulled out,' Ashley tells me.

In the same vein, Paula Rizzo says slides should never be too wordy, not just because it wouldn't look pretty on screen, but also because it could distract your investors from hearing the message you want to get across. 'If you're saying something different than what's on the slide, it's confusing for the viewer. I don't know if I should be listening to what you're saying, or if I should be reading the quote on the screen. So you want to make sure that everything you say is aligned, and that those slides actually complement what you're saying. If you're saying something different than what's on the slide, it's confusing for the viewer. I don't know if I should be listening to what you're saying, or if I should be reading the quote on the screen. So you want to make sure that everything you say is aligned, and that those slides actually complement what you're saying,' says Paula.

'The worst kinds of pitch decks are the ones with bullet points that are just being read by the presenter,' adds Ray Refundo, a fintech startup founder who established Qwikwire, an invoicing and payments platform for large enterprises, and is now chief of finance and head of strategy of buy now, pay later solutions company 4Gives. 'Have you been to those kinds of presentations? There's nothing more boring than that. The presenter has to understand what it is he or she is presenting. They need to prepare. For every minute they speak, they should have practised that for an hour.'

Lastly, one thing you should never, ever forget, says Ashley, is to do a basic spell-check sweep, because typos are always easily spotted by the audience—and make you lose points with them. Again, it's all about paying attention to the little things, because they contribute to your overall credibility as a startup founder.

SIDEBAR: The Arts that Amplify the Pitch

Just as certain sciences can help startup founders improve their pitch, so can particular art disciplines, as shared with me by a few entrepreneurs, including Jeffrey Rogers and Pascal Finette, who are also facilitators at Singularity University, a 'global learning and innovation community' that offers a number of business programmes focused on scaling, strategy, leadership, and the like. According to them, taking up improvisational theatre training can help you become more spontaneous when pitching.

'Pitching is not about perfection; it's about being able to roll with imperfection, because you know that problems are going to pop up. You know that mistakes will be made, and you can make a really strong impression on people when they see how you roll with something that doesn't go according to plan,' says Jeffrey, principal facilitator at SingularityU.

'In theatre, you learn a lot about your stage presence—how do you actually use the stage as an instrument that you can play now? Like, where do you position yourself on stage? How do you position your body towards the audience?' Pascal adds.

Of course, preparation is still key: to be able to improvise, you have to know your material by heart and rehearse it enough that you can play around with it while still being fluid with your pitch's flow.

A more unconventional story on art influencing the ability to pitch comes from Vincent Lau, one of the first participants of *The Final Pitch* in its maiden season.

'When you're pitching on TV and in front of investors, it is very nerve-racking; but it actually brought me back to that time when I was learning classical piano with a focus on performing arts, from when I was age five until eighteen. I just kept telling myself, this is normal, you know, being nervous, being a little tense,' Vincent recalls. 'So I'd say having that kind of formal performing arts training through classical piano, I can't emphasize enough how much that actually helped me. After coming back from the show, I went to my piano teacher—this very strict Taiwanese classical piano champion—and I said, thank you so much, your training actually prepared me so much for *The Final Pitch*.'

The Q&A

We've covered your thinking process for the pitch (science) and how to add flair to the presentation (art), but there's a third part to pitching that can be a bit tricky to prepare for: the questions and answers part. It can be daunting, especially when you're being grilled by multiple investors. Sometimes, according to Amra Naidoo, this bit is what can even potentially sour your pitch—if you aren't ready, and if you don't see it as a chance to get constructive feedback. So, her first piece of advice for facing the Q&A is: don't be defensive.

'I've seen some pretty average or even bad pitches, but they weren't as memorable as the ones who responded really negatively to the questions that were asked,' says Amra, co-founder of the early-stage venture capital fund Accelerating Asia. 'I think a lot of people get defensive when people are asking questions, and I've seen a lot of pitches ruined by what happens during the Q&A. There is actually no need to get defensive; treat it as an opportunity to just get into the details. Assume everyone is curious and not out to tear you down.'

In the experience of Patrick Gentry, co-founder of SaaS startup Sprout, which offers HR management and payroll solutions in the Philippines, going through an accelerator such as Acceleprise in Silicon Valley helped him 'take the heat' during pitching, especially since he and his co-founder and wife Alex had quite the mentor: Ash Rust, managing partner of Sterling Road, a pre-seed venture fund that is also focused on coaching startup founders.

'Ash Rust was our best and most critical mentor. One time I was pitching to him and he was like, "Don't look at me. Why are you looking at me? You're looking at me like you're asking me if what you're saying is okay. You don't need my validation; you're telling me why your company is the best and why I should be lucky to invest in you. Why are you asking me for validation with your eyes?"' Patrick recalls.

Patrick does add the caveat that this kind of training might be more useful to startup pitching in the US market, where investors are more aggressive. 'Having VCs who are brutally honest is very, very useful because it shows you the holes in your business, the holes in your pitch.

As painful as it is at the time, it helps hone you,' Patrick says. On the other hand, given that he and Alex are exposed as well to the Asian market, Patrick says Asian investors tend to be 'very, very nice'—and then surprise you by saying that they are not going to invest.

In terms of preparing yourself for possible questions, Carlo Calimon, director of Philippines-based incubator Startup Village, says the difficult ones that investors will likely ask are about a startup's financials, team members and product-market fit. Sometimes, though, questions could also revolve around specific issues spotted by investors during the pitch that the founder or his team simply didn't see. He calls these 'curveball' questions, because if you knock 'em out of the park, so to speak, then you most likely have a winning pitch.

Combining Art and Science in the Pitch

Ultimately, there is no clear-cut technique that can help you craft the 'perfect' pitch—because perfection isn't the goal; it's all about finding the best investor-partner that can help your company grow. And for that, Anuj Jain of Startup-O advises startup founders to be both left- and right-brained when pitching.

'Painting a picture gives a great vision—emotions and storytelling—but, your investor needs to understand the financial perspective, too,' says Anuj. 'So the pitch is a combination of art and science, naturally, because today's investors want to be part of the journey of something that is changing the world, that is solving real, concrete problems, and has a scalability embedded to it. So from this perspective, you need to think: Who are you pitching to? Focus on the story, and back that up with numbers.'

Presenting the good along with the bad will also serve to strengthen the pitch, says Plentina Co-founder and Chief Business Officer Earl Valencia.

'Why could it fail? What are the risks? I think those are always good conversations, because it shows how you prepare, and that turns out to be a good practical roadmap,' says Earl, who also teaches Digital Transformation, Entrepreneurship, and Innovation as an adjunct faculty member of the Asian Institution of Management in the Philippines.

And whether they stick to a science or are more artsy with their pitch, Earl believes entrepreneurs' strongest suit lies in how much they believe in the business they've built.

'Pitch what you believe in. That's why entrepreneurs keep firing regardless of whether they're successful or not. When they talk to you about their company and why they're building something, it's very difficult. But know that they're doing it because of their own fundamental belief that the world should be better with this new model. And I think that's what makes entrepreneurs amazing,' says Earl.

Chapter Assignments

The science of the pitch deals with how we prepare ourselves mentally and physically for pitch day. Thus, I personally find it beneficial to make time for a quick workout every day to keep myself sharp and on my A-game at all times. I understand, however, that not everyone has the time to exercise every day, so here's an assignment you can try:

- Next time you have calls that you need to take that don't need you to be in front of a computer, string them together in one complete hour block and take the calls while walking. This is the ultimate productivity hack for busy go-getters who want to stay fit.

It's also key to help yourself create a better narrative about your startup, which you can do so by:

- Formulating your story using the Hero's Journey without losing the important elements, such as those listed in the Pitch Canvas. Share that story with your team, and work on refining it for a pitch.
- Getting your team in on the fun by creating a Demo Day Deck, an Email Deck and a Meeting Deck, as described by Caya of Slidebean.

- Practising your video pitch. Apply the pieces of advice you learnt from this chapter and create a one to two-minute video pitch. Afterwards, watch the video and review how you did. What aspects turned out well? What do you need to improve on in terms of facial expressions, non-verbal communication, voice, and tone?
- Speaking in front of a virtual audience. On the next online event or webinar you join, don't just melt into the background. Instead, deliberately make an effort to ask a question or offer a comment during the open forum. Use the opportunity to practise effectively expressing yourself during a video call with an actual virtual audience.

Discussion and due diligence with investor judge William Tiu Lim and his entrepreneur picks

Too short! Entrepreneurs receiving fashion advice right before the pitch finale

John gives a pep talk to the entrepreneurs before the finale

Traditional huddle before *The Final Pitch*

Chapter 6: Pitching to Anyone, Anywhere

Whether through Zoom or at an actual boardroom, your business pitch arsenal, so to speak, is now packed with the most essential information you need for pitch day: the different types of pitches, the topics to cover, how to present yourself, and the elements that best go into a pitch deck. The next challenge is to recognize the different personalities you'll be facing during a pitch. From 'Angels', venture capitalists, private equity, Series A, B, C funding—the list and levels of funding sources can be dizzying, especially to startups that are still getting their feet wet in the ecosystem. Like life, a startup company goes through different stages, and this is what determines the funding source that best suits your business.

Across all types of investors in whatever part of the world, however, it is best to equip yourself with the right knowledge on what exactly they want.

The Essential Qualities of a Startup Founder, According to Investors

According to Jeffrey Seah, partner for the Asia Fund at Quest Ventures, investors are keen on these characteristics when scrutinizing a startup founder:

- Has strength, integrity and honesty;
- Is clear-minded and focused;
- Knows the 'how' and 'why' of the promises they make, and the problem they are trying to solve;
- Is authentic;
- Is vision driven;
- Adheres to value-based leadership;
- Understands the marketplace; and
- Is extremely sensitive to changes.

In the same breath, Jeffrey says a red flag for investors is when someone appears to be joining the startup world just because they see it as something trendy. 'When I look at people, I want to make sure they do not just want to be sexily modern, or be in the tech industry,' says Jeffrey. 'I want to see their mission and vision.'

On top of these qualities, Plentina Chief Business Officer Earl Valencia, an advisor to Silicon Valley tech startups and incubators (aside from being a startup founder himself), says that investors, the 'financial decision makers', like to work with the 'doers'. And to identify just who these doers are, Earl says investors can be expected to ask these questions:

- Why are you in the industry you are in?
- Why is your business important to customers?
- How many customers have you spoken to about your startup, and what did they say about it?

'I want to know that you know more about your industry and the nuances of it. For example, if you're pitching agriculture or healthcare, I would love to understand why, No. 1, it's important to the world, and, No. 2, it's important to the actual customer that you're serving,' Earl explains. 'If I ask, how many customers do you have, and the answer is zero, then that's really bad. That's really bad. There are so many startup entrepreneurs who go into business without even talking to any customer, or even just talking to their friends first. I want to see what the customer sees. If I were to invest in your company, I would at least want to see your prototype on their screens.'

Establishing Trust

Even if you tick all the boxes as the 'ideal' startup founder for investors, why would anyone—a person, a company, an institution—take any risk on you and agree to give you funding in the first place?

Simple: That investor trusts you. Quest Ventures' Jeffrey Seah, for one, says 60 to 70 per cent of the time, he bases his first impression of a startup founder he has just met on his instincts, which are guided by psychological concepts he learnt in his experience as an ad man years ago, before he decided to join the VC world.

'I try to understand the person behind the person. I apply some profiling; I ask questions. Maybe years of profiling customers in the advertising world allowed me to see that, gauging if clients have a $1 million budget, or $10 million. You need to evaluate and be a good judge of people. That's a prerequisite to being a VC,' Jeffrey says.

According to Victor Chua, who is part of the Malaysian Venture Capital and Private Equity Development Council and board member of several tech companies in Southeast Asia, some startup founders simply have the ability to attract support and get people to have faith in them and the work they do. To achieve that, he says, founders should find that balance between transparency and humility, so they can properly inform their investors about their accomplishments. They likewise need to make sure that their numbers are always aligned.

'If we don't have enough data, information or insight on what you are doing and who you are as a person, then we wouldn't know what to act upon,' Victor explains. 'And if your numbers don't add up, that's a red flag, because if, as an entrepreneur, you can't even get your numbers right, how am I going to trust you with the money?'

Establishing a good relationship with your investors, then, even before you actually pitch, would be a great course of action, says Carbon Equity founder Jacqueline Van den Ende, the Dutch entrepreneur who established Lamudi in the Philippines. Throughout her career,

Jacqueline has continually shifted from entrepreneur to investor, giving her a well-rounded perspective of the startup ecosystem.

'Try to create this conscious mindset that you have to play the long game,' she says. 'You need to have multiple conversations. If you look beyond that single moment, that single pitch, as "make or break", you take the pressure off it. Tell yourself, this is one of many pitches, that this is a learning opportunity.'

What Jacqueline means by this is that entrepreneurs need to treat every meeting, no matter how informal, with a potential investor, as an opportunity to simply, well, talk, because it is during these conversations that you will be able to slowly, but surely, build those long-term relationships. These conversations need to be free-flowing, and not come of as a sales meeting, so you can better establish rapport with your potential investors and build your network along the way as well.

Pascal Finette and Jeffrey Rogers, the duo behind the be radical Group, pretty much say the same thing: create a relationship with your potential investor first before pitching. Those relationships, they say, create a network for you, and with a good network comes good opportunities. This also allows you to establish your credibility as a startup founder, and improves your luck in finding the right investor for your company.

The Right Investors, from Seed to Series

Choosing your investors

'When is the right time to pitch to an investor?'

This was one of the recurring questions that popped up in my conversations with the subject matter experts I interviewed for this book, and one of the most interesting responses I received came from Paul Rivera, a 2021 World Economic Forum Young Global Leader and the Filipino entrepreneur who founded careers site Kalibrr: raise money when you don't need to.

Paul explains: 'A mistake I've often made—and kind of everyone has—is to raise money only when we need to, or else the company's gonna die. We're gonna die in one month, three months, six months, right? So you're always raising from a position of very little leverage, unless you know you're dying, but still growing really quickly your users and your revenue. That's a little bit different. So, the best time to raise money is when you don't need to, and it's amazing how the dynamics of the conversation changes, when I'm talking to an investor and I don't need any money. As an investor, their job is to give money, to deploy money. Their job is actually difficult, because if they don't invest, they're literally not doing their job.'

This entails, too, that the best time to raise money is when you've somehow proven your salt as a startup entrepreneur; in other words, it's best to seek funding when you have something to show for your work—traction. It all ties back to that element of trust, and getting investors comfortable enough to finance your goals. Doron Latzer, co-founder and senior partner of Pearl Cohen Zedek Latzer Baratz law firm, also adds that having your core team in place is also strong proof that you are in it for the long haul.

Once you're ready, the next step is to determine the investor that will best help your business grow. Chinaccelerator Managing Director William Bao Bean advises startup founders to 'rank' their potential investors based on their appropriateness for the company and likelihood of closing, then to pitch last to the ones whom they are really eyeing for funding, because by that time, you would've done your pitch enough times and would be more prepared to face your target investors.

Pitching, ultimately, should be viewed as a sales effort, too, says Mohan Belani, mentor at Founder Institute, the world's largest startup accelerator for those in the pre-seed stage. You can't just randomly pitch, or wish for an investor to take an interest in you; you have to be clear with your goals and put in the work for yourself into the meetings that matter.

Pitching to venture capitalists

To the uninitiated, Brian Ngan, venture partner at VU Venture Partners and chief investment officer of Cedarside Holdings Corporation explains the advantage of private markets—VCs, private equities (PE)—over going public: 'Private investors are the people with the *quality* network. I emphasize the quality side of it, because I can always ask anyone what he thinks a business is worth and he's just going to give me a useless number; but at the end of the day, it's someone with the competence in your field that can [guide you]. It's also the people who are competent who will tell you upfront where they're not competent in--and that's the beauty of private markets.'

The difference between VCs and PEs, explains Ray Refundo, founder and CEO of FinTech company Qwikwire, is that PEs 'look at everything you learn in school', while VCs 'look at your grand vision'.

'Venture capitalists are betting on the future, and they are betting on you, the founder,' explains Ray. 'They look at trends, too; even if you're not the greatest startup, if you're in the right space at the right time, then it's easier to get funding.'

So, the million-dollar (or billion, depending on what stage your startup is in) question: if you're taking the VC route, where should you even start looking?

It all depends on which stage you are at as a startup. For husband-and-wife business partners Patrick and Alex, the couple behind Philippines-based HR management software company Sprout Solutions, those who are raising their seed round would be best to stick to their local market first, because investors from continents away will likely find it hard to place their money in a startup that is based too far from them.

'We tried so hard to raise our seed round from investors in the US or internationally because I thought, well, it's such a bigger market, it'll be easier to find an investor there,' says Patrick. 'But investors in the US aren't going to invest a seed round in the Philippines, because it's so far.'

The ability to show that your startup has had some form of traction is also highly important during your seed round; as Ray had mentioned, it's your future that matters to them—which means you need to be able to demonstrate a promising one for your company. Traction was the key element that was missing from Patrick and Alex's pitch to a

Singaporean investor whom they pitched to when they were still raising seed money. It also didn't help, says Patrick, that the investor had a poker face that they just couldn't read.

'Alex and I went to a hotel to meet him, and it's incredibly unnerving when a VC is just stone faced. I'm insecure, I need validation,' says Patrick, chuckling together with Alex as he shares their story. 'I had no idea if this guy hates us, if he loves us; I have no idea what's going on in his head. Alex and I are both very intuitive and we're able to read people super well, but it was like this guy was playing *Texas Hold 'Em* at some big tournament in Las Vegas or something. And I was sweating and freaking out and doing a horrible job pitching Sprout. We got up from that table saying, "We are never gonna hear from that guy."'

They didn't—for a while. They met again after a few months, when Patrick and Alex were raising their Series A, and the timing was finally right for both parties. 'He had seen us grow a lot in the last six months, and, basically, his perspective was, "Oh wow, these guys aren't just full of it; and they're really growing." It was a better deal for him,' Patrick says. 'And the other thing was—he liked us! He just didn't express it, at the time.'

What Patrick and Alex have also learnt is that the right investor isn't hard to pitch to, and that if they're asking questions that seem bizarre or not in line with your startup, then they probably aren't the right one for you.

As described by Steve Sy, founder of Great Deals, an e-commerce enabler based in the Philippines, it's the 'uncomplicated' investors that you want to deal with, especially since you will be giving up some control over your business once they enter the picture. For Steve, that uncomplicated investor, for their Series A funding, was Manila-based private equity firm Navegar, from which Great Deals received a whopping $12 million—and in the middle of a pandemic, at that.

'It was uncomplicated because it was straight up equity,' Steve says. 'There were no other conditions, like liquidation, reference; and I was able to negotiate what I wanted because I knew my business could grow and scale. I told them, we're a very unique company, we're an earning company with these revenues, and we have so many things that are going for us, being in the sunrise industry of e-commerce.'

Moreover, Steve, whose success with Great Deals has led him to branch to other industries—his newest venture is online farm-to-kitchen marketplace Zagana—says as long as startup founders focus on growing their businesses, finding VCs and PEs that will support them through their Series B, C funding (and beyond) will become easier and easier.

'By the time Series B rolled in, Great Deals had its pick of investors—because from 2019 to 2020, we grew the company by four times. And how many companies can say that they grew by that much in the middle of a pandemic?' Steve says.

Something to keep in mind: maintaining control

When getting an investor on board to grow your startup, lawyer Mark Gorriceta of Gorriceta Africa Cauton & Saavedra advises startups to maintain majority, or 51 per cent, of the control over the business—otherwise, he says the transaction already falls under the M&A (mergers and acquisitions) category. Founders who want to continue running day-to-day operations as the president need to convey this clearly to their investors.

The number of board seats investors get is another matter to consider, since board members direct company policies. 'If they want a seat on the board, it should be commensurate with their percentage of holdings,' advises Mark, a top tech lawyer in the Philippines whose legal expertise revolves around capital markets, M&A, taxation, and corporate law. According to him, for a five-seat board, 20 per cent ownership equates to one board seat. 'It all depends how much you're asking for; if you are asking for so much, then they would also ask a lot from you. If you really want to have control then, retain two-thirds of the board, which is the super majority. You can also identify through the shareholders agreement what items would remain within your power.'

When an angel comes along

Like a gift from above, sometimes, someone comes along and helps startup founders get on their feet, banking not on their traction, but merely their potential. These are the 'angels', startup founders' saving grace.

How exactly can you identify someone as your angel investor? As explained by Joseph de Leon and Artie Lopez of the Manila Angel Investors Network, angel investors give founders their first funding, entering the picture when the business is still in its very early stages. VCs, as we discussed earlier, invest after you've already had your first round of funding.

In the case of Great Deals' Steve Sy, his angel investor was a trusted friend—someone who simply trusted in him enough to provide him funding even if he didn't have a financial statement to present back then.

Angels also differ from VCs in terms of:

- Check size. VCs invest more than angels; however, a caveat, says Joseph, is that the amount that angel investors put in would also depend on the region where you are located. For example, angels in the US would have more financial bandwidth compared to those, say, in Southeast Asia.
- Portfolio mix. Joseph explains that in terms of their portfolio, VCs go for optionality by diversifying their risk while angels' gun for asymmetry. 'Angels would invest ideally when they know something that the market doesn't, or they have unique access that the market doesn't,' Joseph says.

Joseph and Artie warn, however, that sometimes, pitching to angel investors, especially a syndicate of angels, could prove to be tricky—if your startup plan isn't solid enough. 'A syndicate of angels can be harsher because you can't bullshit a high network of individuals who built businesses from scratch,' says Joseph. 'On the flip side, a VC's job is to listen because they have a quota per month. They would never shut you down or turn you down off the bat because they may want to invest later.'

Other Funding Sources

To bootstrap or to borrow?

Our previous discussions focused on funding from investors, or external resources who, in exchange for their infusion of capital in your business, would have a stake in it as well. However, some startup founders, especially those who have yet to build their network, take to bootstrapping or simply relying on their own resources in order to grow their enterprise.

And based on a true story, which I share below, relayed to me by Ambassador Benedicto Yujuico, president of the Philippine Chamber of Commerce and Industry, there is definitely virtue to starting an enterprise from the ground up.

I met Ambassador Yujuico when I was nominated for an entrepreneurship award named after Injap Sia, the young entrepreneur behind Mang Inasal, a highly popular roasted chicken fast-food chain in the Philippines, and the story I always associate with bootstrapping is about Injap—specifically, the first time Ambassador Yujuico met him, over a decade ago in Colombo, Sri Lanka.

Injap was, at that time, a young thirty-something entrepreneur who had grown Mang Inasal to more than 300 stores. When they opened their first branches, Mang Inasal became a crowd favourite among Filipinos because of their unlimited extra rice offering, with the wait staff even going around the diners to serve rice to customers asking for seconds and thirds. Ambassador Yujuico and Injap were in Colombo then, in an event where the latter had been nominated for the third Asia Pacific Young Entrepreneur Award of the Confederation of Asia-Pacific Chambers of Commerce and Industry (CACCI)—which Ambassador Yujuico was president of back then—alongside other successful entrepreneurs from across the region.

Ambassador Yujuico believed Injap to be a strong contender, given his accomplishments—and was completely surprised that the award went instead to a Sri Lankan entrepreneur.

'I asked the chairman of that awards committee, hey can you tell me why he didn't win? And he said they couldn't really decide—until they finally had to ask one question: how did you get the money to start your business?' says Ambassador Yujuico.

Apparently, Injap took out a P2,000,000 loan from his father, who at that time owned a grocery. On the other hand, the winner, Nayana Dehigama of the Epic Lanka Group, bootstrapped his enterprise—the deciding factor behind his win.

The point of Ambassador Yujuico's story isn't to discourage anyone from taking out loans or going after investors for their startups; after all, these are options that can help entrepreneurs scale faster. 'Injap may not have come from humble beginnings, but he was able to use the P2-million loan wisely to grow one of the biggest fast-food chains in the Philippines, which was later acquired by another fast-food giant Jollibee for the sum of P3 billion,' says Ambassador Yujuico. 'His forays into real estate with DoubleDragon Properties have made him one of the wealthiest men in the Philippines, and the IPO of his grocery chain MerryMart during the pandemic bucked trends and pushed his valuation even higher—all this from a P2-million loan he took out from his parents when he was a teenager.'

What borrowing and growing money can give your startup, as exhibited by what Injap experienced, is a competitive edge over other companies, as doing so establishes a founder's ability to make the money he borrowed grow—essentially what an IPO is supposed to promise its stakeholders.

On the other end of the spectrum, Warren Leow, CEO of the Inmagine Group, a company that provides businesses with a creative ecosystem composed of libraries of stock images, editing tools, and design templates, says the opposite holds true for him. Inmagine has been bootstrapped since day one of the businesses.

'There are a few things which have put us on a unique standing—and number one is we are bootstrapped,' says Warren. 'And number two, we are a global company.'

However, bootstrapping also entails that your startup is able to churn a profit, Warren adds as a caveat. Two critical factors also play a role in bootstrapping: a founder's ability to manage the cost of operations and his personal budget, and, well, luck.

'Luck plays an important role, and for Inmagine, we were able to push it through because the timing was right—and the product was right, too,' Warren says. 'It took a few years, but Inmagine eventually grew.'

Family, friends, fools

Across the world, the impact of family businesses on the global GDP is over 70 per cent. One family business expert here in the Philippines, professor Enrique Soriano III, or Prof. Eric, to those who know him closely, knows too well the huge impact that family has on how businesses are run; in fact, he has made it his life's mission to enable family-run enterprises all over the world to grow and succeed, working as a consultant who helps them navigate personal and professional issues that naturally overlap among families that are running a business. After all, nothing makes for better drama than family members bickering over money.

Mainly, Prof. Eric, executive director of the Wong+Bernstein Advisory Group, who also teaches at the Ateneo Graduate School of Business, manages the generational differences between the business' founder, and his or her children and grandchildren, and how the older generations shoot down new business ideas when pitched to them by, essentially, their heirs. As I had mentioned earlier in Chapter 2: Knowing Your 'Why' and Finding Your 'Who', Prof. Eric advises the younger generations of family-run companies, first and foremost, to build credibility among their elders, especially those sceptical of change. Simply showing up to the office before or at exactly 8 a.m., says Prof Eric, would establish that much-needed trust between older and younger generations, since the former would be able to appreciate any new ideas more if he or she can see that his or her successor is putting in the hard work.

'Unless the next generation puts in the time and effort to build that credibility, they will have a hard time pitching great concepts and great ideas. But the moment the senior generation accepts them as a hardworking member of the company, then it would be easier for them to pitch new ideas,' says Prof. Eric.

Prof. Eric also shares these tips for younger-generation family members who want to establish new processes and systems in their family-run businesses (a common phenomenon he says he has seen amid the pandemic, given the strong demand for companies to go digital):

- The older generation is direct to the point. Keep the pitch short and sweet. Older members want to know where the revenue stream would be, how much the ask is, and how much they'll earn from it, and if there would be equity.
- For bigger corporations, investing in the second generation is not a problem because they've set aside capital expenditure for new businesses.
- Senior businessmen are very opportunistic; they would make sure that they own the majority. They'll be more comfortable if they're the majority, especially for businesses they're familiar with. Some may be comfy with having a third of the control, but they must have a say in the business.

For startups who are simply seeking a bit of financial help from family and friends, the founder's reputation and relationship with these people are key, says Roland Ros, founder of livestreaming platform Kumu, who says his first investment for his now extremely popular business came from his own pocket, plus the $300,000 or so given by friends and family. 'Your entrepreneurial journey is going to be riddled with a bunch of failures and wins, and the number one thing that you cannot put a price on is your reputation and this track record of trust that you built throughout the years. When you're at that initial friends-and-family funding round, they are going to invest in the founder, not in the business idea; my friends and family helped me because these are people who have been with me over the last five to ten years, and I've done business with them, saw lots of tears lots of struggles and a lot of successes with them—and I never burned bridges.'

However, Podcast Network Asia founder, Ron Baetiong, also shares this little nugget of wisdom when it comes to seeking financial help from family and friends. It's a strategy that works best only when you're surrounded by people who actually have the means to help you out. Otherwise, as Ron puts it, startup founders need to 'punch higher than their weight class', just as he did, so he could build the relationships he needed—i.e., investors—to get his business up and running.

Corporates, conglomerates

Aside from bootstrapping, taking out a loan either from family or a financial institution, or getting the buy-in of investors, corporations and conglomerates are also now a viable funding source for startups. The larger, more traditional companies that used to rule the business world now see the value of investing in startups and the disruptive ideas they create to cater to consumers' evolving needs and wants. Still, as with any investor, corporations and conglomerates won't be pouring any funding into something they don't see as a worthwhile investment. Supachai 'Kid' Parchariyanon, CEO and co-founder of RISE, which works with corporations and governments with the mission to 'lift up Thailand and Southeast Asia' through their corporate innovation platform, dishes out these tips for those pitching to these larger entities:

- Be clear with your key value proposition and address the corporate's pain points. 'Startups have been popping up in the past years and most of the time, corporations would love to work with them, to help them. If you are clear on that value proposition, most of the time, you'll be able to score with corporate investors.'
- Make good use of corporate investors' time, because the key people in corporations are always busy.
- Have your MVP or basic business plan ready for presentation before approaching corporate investors.
- Mindset alignment is also important. Startups and corporations both need to move fast, especially the latter, because startups

produce technology quickly. This is why Kid advises startups to 'look for partnerships'—corporate investors that they can go on a ride together with, and not those who would just squeeze their margins.

- Lastly, the partnership should be one that is win-win-win—for the corporation, the startup and, of course, the end users.

Government support

While perhaps not as agile as private investors, government partnerships are also another way for startups to secure the funding that they need to scale. In Malaysia, for one, government support for the startup ecosystem is felt through the budget they allot for universities developing new technology and intellectual property, shares Herman Syah Abdul Rahim, principal and senior vice president of Kumpulan Modal Perdana (KMP), a technology VC wholly owned by the country's Ministry of Finance, and is also under the Ministry of Science, Technology & Innovation (MOSTI).

Malaysian government-backed Cradle Fund has also been a strong enabler of the country's tech startups, having funded over 900 of these companies over the past fifteen years. Adam Ramskay, head of strategy at Cradle, says they help startups by equipping them with the right tools that they can use to add value to their business, whether it's through study sessions, knowledge-building programmes, peer-to-peer support, providing market access, or taking them to the global stage. 'At Cradle, we believe funding is just one part of the equation in growing startups,' Adam explains. 'The other part is the support they can get so they can take their business to the next level. Most startups are just starting out in business, so they may not have the right knowledge or the right experience. This is where we come in.'

In the Philippines, one similar partnership is being run under a programme called QBO (pronounced 'kubo', which is the term for the traditional Filipino hut) has been building the local startup ecosystem for years by working with both the private and public sector, with the country's Department of Trade and Industry and Department of Science and Technology as their main government allies.

Katrina Rausa Chan, IdeaSpace Foundation executive director, specifically identifies what startups stand to gain from a government partnership:

- Government has the machinery to create big changes in the startup ecosystem. 'Government is the only real entity that can take a startup initiative and make it a national programme. There's a certain inertia behind government support; yes, it takes a while, but once it makes a move, it does so in big ways.'

- Government invests in research. Kat makes an example of Silicon Valley and Sta. Clara Valley. Before they became the world's premier tech and startup hubs, they were the largest recipients of US federal grant funding on research.

- Government is in it for the long haul. QBO's efforts, which include their Technology Business Incubator 4.0 initiative that provides Filipino startups with development programmes, may not have immediate payoff, but Kat explains that over time, it's these kinds of programmes that help build a density of entrepreneurs and ideas.

Grants

Grants are another funding source that can be greatly beneficial to startups, and these can be found in the impact investment space. According to Amra Naidoo, Asia Pacific lead for shaper impact capital and outgoing curator for the Global Shapers Singapore Hub, an initiative of the World Economic Forum, some startups don't need to go the VC route, and can opt for grants first.

'Many of the companies that we're working with are addressing a Sustainable Development Goal,' says Amra, who is also co-founder of Accelerating Asia and general partner at Accelerating Asia Ventures. 'We often encourage them to apply for grants. It's so efficient on the cap table, as many of these development organizations providing grants are very excited to be working with social impact startups.'

She also debunks a preconceived notion she has typically encountered among startups when it comes to social impact grants: that such organizations cannot really make money while doing good.

'I hate that school of thought because it assumes that business is bad, that there's a fundamental assumption that a business must be destroying everything for it to work. Many of the entrepreneurs don't know about the whole social impact space. They are literally out there to solve a problem for their markets and they come up with a business model about social impact by nature,' says Amra.

With that said, Amra advises startups to highlight their social impact when pitching for these kinds of grants—and how they can actually achieve those goals.

Pitch Competition: The Showtime Effect

I may be biased, but pitching on a reality TV show is, in my opinion, one of the most effective and high-impact strategies to raise funding and awareness for a startup. There is a very tangible and unique benefit to pitching on reality TV show, something I call the Showtime Effect.

The Showtime Effect is the net positive push of factors present in a televised pitch that makes the pitch more likely to succeed as opposed to if it were not televised.

Think about it. The producers have carefully chosen you to make sure that you are a good fit. Before you even open your mouth to greet the judges, everyone—from the producers to the judges to the guy who mops the floor on the set—is rooting for you. You are pitching to the judges but there are thousands if not millions of people who will see your pitch—your next pool of potential customers, investors and fans.

The judges, since you may be thinking otherwise, are not there to give you a hard time and to tear your pitch apart. They genuinely want you to be good and regret every time someone just ends up wasting their time. So it is also in their best interest to make sure that a deal, if you are a good fit and they like you, gets done.

At the end of the day, the audience will get their adrenaline rush when the hero lands the deal. Anything less than that is an opportunity to show the audience a lesson. It's showtime, and you are now a vessel to teach people either how to do it or how not to do it.

The extreme case is, of course, inviting you in because you just suck so bad. 'It's so bad it's good' quickly became the formula for the singing show *American Idol* until it got old and repetitive. The infamous William Hung is the classic example of someone who was not supposed to be there, but because he clearly believed that his out of tune rendition of Ricky Martin's hit song *She Bangs* was singing, he became a viral sensation and an instant phenomenon. It didn't stop him from releasing three albums and even his very own movie. He eventually retired from music, and is an occasional motivational speaker. In a *Variety* article (22 September 2020), when asked how he felt about the way he was received by the judges when he auditioned way back in 2004, William said, 'The way I saw the judges, I felt like they were just playing their roles. So that's why I didn't feel the need to be angry or upset.'

You must also be aware that the judges are there not just to find entrepreneurs to invest in, but to also put on a show.

It is in everyone's best interest for a deal to get done, but as producers of the show, it is also in our best interest to make sure there are 'teaching moments' that allow for our audience to learn something.

In the event that a deal does not push through on the show, the long tail of people having watched you on TV pitch your heart out has very tangible benefits, as attested to by Ray Refundo, CEO and founder of Qwikwire.

'When Qwikwire started out, it was hard to get clients. After *The Final Pitch*—and, as you know clients Google you when you pitch to them—once they saw all that content about us pitching on the show, it gave us more credibility, and our clients became more comfortable in partnering with us,' Ray recalls.

What Podcast Network Asia Founder Ron Baetiong highly appreciated about joining a show like *The Final Pitch* was how it connected him directly to investors and 'what startups actually need—funding'. Based on his experience, he advises startups that are applying to join a reality TV competition to do their homework and research the investor-judges, and to also be prepared to totally lose their momentum in the middle of their pitch.

'I'm typically a momentum kind of guy, but when we were filming that last episode, there were planes flying overhead, so we just needed to keep cutting and cutting—and it's easy to lose your flow,' Ron recalls. Despite that, Ron was able to zero in on the investors he wanted, and learnt how to be precise with his pitch during the show.

'I'm not gonna waste my time trying to pitch bricks; when you say pitching bricks, this is people that don't even have the ability to be attracted to what I will say. I researched the four judges, and I focused on the two people that I wanted to work with. Eventually, they were the ones who picked me,' Ron says.

But it's not just the entrepreneurs who got a leg up during the show; some of the investor-judges themselves experienced a business boost by joining the show. Mica Tan, the millennial CEO behind the MFT Group of Companies, says *The Final Pitch* helped humanize her company, and enabled them to attract better talent.

'We've been able to reach a wider network of executives and other talent all across the organization, who want to be part of the organization because of what they saw on the show,' says Mica.

Michael Dargani, President and CEO of IceDream, Inc., the official licensee of Baskin Robbins in the Philippines, also credits the prominence his business received—and the opportunities they've discovered—to their exposure on *The Final Pitch*. Before the show, we didn't know each other personally, and he had no idea about the show, either.

'I value my privacy. But we had good rapport and it was a good opportunity,' Michael tells me. 'We happened to meet at a conference; only one seat was available, and it was the one next to you. Destiny, I guess—we exchanged cards, and I was looking for investment opportunities. No thought of being part of the show, because I didn't know how to do that. But I'm really glad that I did because it has opened up a lot of opportunities for me.'

Location, Location, Location – Yes, It Matters

Wherever you are in the world, you can find an investor who can help your startup take off; however, for most startup founders, the holy grail, so to speak, for startup pitching can be found in Silicon Valley, the home of many prominent tech institutions. For any founder, just merely pitching within the region is an achievement in itself. Who wouldn't want to have Facebook, Apple, and Google pixie dust rub off on them?

According to investor and CEO Chris Peralta, most startups who head to the southern San Francisco Bay Area are in it for two reasons: first, access to scale the business, and second, to raise funds. However, not every startup is in the right position to pitch there.

'A lot of the time, they're not ready to come to Silicon Valley at all,' Chris says. 'First, they haven't even established themselves locally in the market and they're not ready to scale.'

Chris also believes that not having a presence in Silicon Valley may lower your chances of getting funding from investors in the bay area. But sometimes, giving it a try is all it takes—even if the odds are stacked against you.

SIDEBAR: Pitching in Silicon Valley

2013. When Kalibrr co-founder and CEO Paul Rivera was raising funds for his skills development platform startup, he deliberately didn't apply to Y Combinator, the Mountain View-based accelerator that launched Airbnb, Stripe, DoorDash, and over 2,000 other startups.

'I was never gonna get in; YC was primarily focused on US-based startups,' Paul tells me years later.

Upon raising funds from their first institutional investor, Paul plucked up the courage to fly to the Valley to get more money, but not from YC.

'After about fifty meetings, no one committed. One of the meetings I had was with Sam Altman, who became the first president of YC. And I was pitching to him as an angel, and he said, 'You should take that YC application, it's due in four days,' Paul recounts. 'We were never getting it in, it's not worth the effort. But, you know, I'm in the Valley, and I might as well apply.'

With the deadline fast-approaching, he filled out the application and submitted a thirty-minute video—twenty-nine minutes in excess of the required running time. Despite applying last minute and not adhering to the requirement rules, they got in.

'It was a ten-minute interview with four or five partners. There was no format. They could ask anything. It was like a thesis,' Paul recalls.

'It was a very lively debate. The questions could be seen as dismissive—"Call centres? Why are there call centres in the Philippines?"—but they were trying to understand. And so I think the lesson there that I give to people during pitch interviews is to just know your problem space; you know that better than anyone.'

Going through an unstructured, free-for-all 'defence' was exhausting. But before the day ended, an email made it all worth it.

'Later that night, they said, we got it.'

If you're intent on packing your bags and booking a flight to the West Coast to raise funds, you need to develop a thick skin. As illustrated by Paul's experience, you need to be prepared for 'dismissive' questions. There's a big chance that you'll get blunt feedback, or on your worst day, savage comments that cut.

Jojo Flores, co-founder of Silicon Valley-based accelerator and incubator Plug and Play, knows how Asian founders could find it difficult to pitch in the West. As a Filipino living in the US, he's very well aware of the cultural nuances.

'The general way of business in the West is direct while in the east it's not confrontational and based on relationships,' Jojo tells me. 'Our nos and yeses don't really mean what they should mean. It's simpler in the West, what you see is what you get.'

Sprout co-founders and married couple Patrick and Alex Gentry are no strangers to Silicon Valley. Aside from having pitched to YC themselves, they've also gone through the programme of Acceleprise, a startup accelerator that focuses on helping startups that provide businesses with Software-as-a-Service (SaaS).

They told me about how intense the programme was. Brutally honest investors who sat at their pitches made the experience even more unnerving.

'We were in the accelerator and it was very hot that day,' Patrick tells me. 'It was in the middle of summer and the AC wasn't working properly. This room was really stuffy and these three sweaty investors were sitting there at the table and I was presenting Sprout.'

'And when I got to the valuation, they were like, "That valuation is crazy. You're ridiculous." Something along those lines and just said no,' he continued, chuckling. 'I didn't know what to say, or how to act. I was just pouring sweat, and it was just incredibly nerve-wracking.'

'The whole experience was meant to take you out of your comfort zone,' Alex chimes in. 'There's a whole section of the programme that was all about controlling the room, the power dynamics.'

'That intense training would be more needed in the US market where investors are a lot more aggressive,' Patrick added. 'Having VCs who are brutally honest is very, very useful because it shows you the holes in your business and in your pitch. As painful as it is at the time, it helps hone you.'

Aggressive as it is, one great thing about Silicon Valley startup culture is that it provides a level playing field to anyone with the chops and determination. In fact, a cold pitch may even be fruitful if you had the credentials to back it up.

'Everyone is willing to kind of help everyone out, even if you're kind of a nobody,' Paul Rivera remarks. 'A kind of open mentality.'

Pascal Finette, co-founder at management consulting firm Be Radical, told me about how he once sent a cold email to bestselling author and speaker Seth Godin. To his surprise, Seth replied to his email within the same day.

A decade later, Pascal shared the encounter when he and Seth spoke at the same event together.

'I was telling the story that I sent Seth an email ten plus years ago and he responded within two hours. It was a cold email and I was reciting the story on stage just to highlight how amazing Seth Godin is,' Pascal recalls.

'And he says something really fascinating to me. He stopped me in my sentence and said, "Pascal, you didn't send me a cold email—your prior actions earned you the right to send me the email and earned you the right that I respond to you."'

Adopting the Silicon Valley Mindset

The bay area is appealing to entrepreneurs with big dreams, that's for sure. But heading to the land of opportunity isn't a requirement to grow a startup. In fact, Paul Rivera says innovations involving funding have brought a myriad of alternatives to the path he took pitching in the Valley in 2013.

'What you should try to get is the mindset. Silicon Valley, I think, is really more of a mindset,' Paul says. 'It's a set of principles, the right way to make decisions. A way to build a company, a way to interact with other people. Have a mindset of not blindly taking risks, but deliberately taking calculated risks with your career decisions, and deciding if it makes sense at some point.'

According to MobKard founder and CEO Carlo Calimon, it's all about looking at Silicon Valley's best practices and applying what works in one's local startup ecosystem.

Carlo is also the director of StartUp Village, an idea-stage incubator in the Philippines. They organized excursions to Silicon Valley to expose entrepreneurs to the way business is done in the bay area, and my wife, Monica, and I were able to join one of these trips back in late 2018.

'I think it's more of drawing inspiration and adopting what's relevant for you . . . There are collaborations and partnerships among the participants. It's the vibe,' Carlo said about the Silicon Valley excursions. 'And remember, when you're happy and excited, the more you retain memory.'

Southeast Asian Startup Ecosystem

The startup ecosystem in Southeast Asia may not be as mature as that of Silicon Valley, but it's definitely thriving. Adam Ramskay, strategy and venture development manager at Malaysia's early-stage startup influencer Cradle Fund sees one particular entity that invigorated the regional ecosystem: the ride-booking app MyTeksi launched by Anthony Tan in 2012.

'They received funding from us twice. Initially they got a grant of MYR 150,000 ($35,490), they started off with that and once they've reached a certain point to scale up, then we've funded them for MYR 500,000 ($118,301),' Adam recalls.

'Once they grew, they were starting to get investors from a whole lot of other people and they decided to establish a business in Singapore. It had a multiplier effect, it has galvanized the rest of the ecosystem.'

Just months after it launched in Malaysia, the startup set up shop in other Southeast Asian cities, including Manila.

'Anthony and Jesse Maxwell, its first Philippine investor, came to me in mid-2012, this is just about four months after the launch in Malaysia and we incorporated here in December 2012,' Foxmont Capital Partners managing partner Franco Varona shares.

MyTeksi is what we now know as Grab and has eventually expanded to offer other services such as food deliveries and courier services. During its early days, the startup helped support livelihoods and boosted local economies. But more than that, it opened up a whole box of possibilities for founders, investors and end users in Southeast Asia. Startups, which used to be met with scepticism in such a traditional region, suddenly looked promising and worth betting on.

SIDEBAR: It Takes Razor-Sharp Focus to Scale Fast

'One thing that Anthony Tan was always very good at was sticking to the core message,' Franco shares with me about his interactions with the Grab founder. Franco was Grab's general manager when it first established its presence in Manila in 2012.

'He always reverts back to one story which is that his grandfather was a taxi driver and that he understood the plight of Malaysian taxi drivers based on what he has grown up with and heard but how hard it was to be a taxi driver. Literally tunnel vision from day one. You just can't talk to him about anything else . . . If you're gonna talk business, you're gonna talk Grab. He's never been distracted.'

So, what exactly makes the Southeast Asian startup ecosystem unique? For one, while most startups in the US are geared towards making the world a better place, Southeast Asian startups are more focused on solving real-world problems. Another difference lies in the purpose behind building a business, which also stems from material conditions.

'I think Asians are actually way more entrepreneurial and have definitely been at the forefront of building businesses and trying out new business models,' Mohan Belani, co-founder and CEO of tech media platform e27 tells me. 'In the US, there's a deeper sense of civic-mindedness—getting involved in activities or activism to keep wanting to do better for society.'

American businesses are busy developing self-driving technologies, blockchain and space transportation because they've already got the essential needs covered. Most Southeast Asian startups, on the other hand, are addressing more fundamental living aspects such as healthcare, education and fintech.

'Southeast Asia has a lot of problems, which also means a lot of opportunities,' Mohan says.

And since a great number of Southeast Asian startups are focused on basic needs, the coronavirus pandemic only allowed them to prove their unique value proposition.

'A lot of startups today, Covid-19 allowed them to pivot really fast,' Jeffrey Seah, a partner at venture capital fund Quest Ventures observes. 'Before, a lot of startups were a bit quirky, but now they are all so mainstream and started becoming mainstream players.'

Pitching in Southeast Asia

Being a mainstream player often means having to raise funds to further expand the business. But how does an entrepreneur do that in such a diverse region as Southeast Asia?

If you're an early-stage startup, it makes sense to approach investors within your country first before going regional. That's the advice of Doron Latzer, Pearl Cohen senior partner who works out of the firm's New York and Tel Aviv offices.

'Early-stage investors usually try to invest in their own territory,' Doron remarks. 'It's very difficult to invest $100,000 anywhere else if you don't know what comes out. It's a trust issue because there's little to show at this stage. So I don't think seeking early-stage investment makes sense if you do it in foreign countries.'

In addition to trust issues, logistics is another reason investors would want to put money in home-grown businesses first.

'Vietnamese investors, they would first prefer the local startups because they want to avoid any barriers in terms of the moving stage and culture,' David Lang, founder and CEO of joint stock company Viettonkin explains. 'But they are more open and receptive to foreign projects which help them grow and scale up because of Covid.'

Southeast Asia is a melting pot of multi-religion, multilingual, and multi-ethnic populations. That being said, doing business in this region boils down to respecting the culture of the country you're in. Before you pitch to investors in another country, it might help to get in touch with someone familiar with the customs and culture so that you don't walk into the room unprepared.

Below are some cultural nuances you might need to be aware of, if you're planning to do cross-border pitching in Southeast Asia.

Traditional businessmen

Unlike in Silicon Valley, where a lot of investors may have been startup founders themselves, it's not surprising to find yourself pitching to more traditional businessmen in Southeast Asia. These are business patriarchs or matriarchs who grew their company from the ground up with blood, sweat and tears.

Bear in mind that there's a difference between how traditional businessmen and startup founders receive and handle pitches.

'Founders love talking about: What is the big vision here? What is your technology differentiation that could get you there?' Earl Valencia, Plentina co-founder and chief business officer says.

'If you talk to someone—regardless if it's East or West—and they're trained in classic finance or private equity, the first thing they'll ask you is metrics: What's your unit economics? How do you really make money?'

In short, while an investor steeped in startup culture might be more appreciative of the founder's vision, traditional businessmen would put more weight on results and what has actually been done. This only goes to show that wherever you are and whoever you're pitching to, you need to organize your data and get your story straight before showing up at the meeting.

Non-confrontational attitude

Asians, in general, don't like confrontation. In fact, blunt comments can be perceived as inappropriate or even rude. Mario Berta, an Italian startup CEO who has pitched in all corners of the world, learnt that he needs to be extra sensitive when pitching to Asian investors.

'Asians are not combative. They don't like to be challenged publicly,' Mario observes. 'In America, you can afford to be pushier like a second-hand car dealer in Texas. You can't afford to do that in Asia because the moment you try to challenge people on the answer, they close up immediately. So you need to be cautious about this.'

Just as they don't want to be at the receiving end of a combative statement, Asians also avoid having to confront anyone. Prof. Eric Soriano, a business educator and World Bank/International Finance Corporation governance consultant, says Asians rarely say no—but not exactly because they're saying yes.

'In most cases, when the client says let's defer this for now, that's pretty much as good as saying no,' Prof. Eric tells me. 'In my experience, maybe one or two would flatly say we don't want to invest. But the rest will be so courteous to simply say, not this time, maybe next year.'

This cultural nuance may spare the founder from a bruised ego. However, there are also obvious downsides. For one, having someone 'defer' their decision on the pitch can leave you stuck in a grey area. Should you count them as investors or not?

In addition to that, you won't likely get the investor's honest feedback, which can be gold when you're trying to develop your startup and hone your pitch.

Humility is shared virtue

Along with being non-confrontational, it's not typical for Southeast Asians to hog the limelight. In fact, humility is a much-valued virtue. Being good at one thing without bragging about it, sometimes even downplaying the achievement a little bit, is the true mark of a refined person.

In the Philippines, for instance, older generations love movies with an action hero who starts off as a vulnerable underdog in the first act, works hard to master his craft during the second act, and gets to showcase his strength and prowess (but only because he has to) during climax. The movie's denouement will paint him as the same humble person he once was—only richer, in a better position in society, and with his dream woman by his side.

Such a film trope would also likely find an audience in Malaysia. Victor Chua, managing partner at Vynn Capital, told me that Malaysians also value humility.

'I don't know if it's right or wrong but Malaysians are too humble,' Victor says. 'Malaysian entrepreneurs are those who do their own work and mind their own business. They believe that if they are a real gem, someone else would be able to find them ... We are not as expressive as peers from Singapore, Philippines and Vietnam as well.'

Facing investors who value humility doesn't necessarily mean you'll need to clam up and pretend to be meek or timid. Like anywhere else, it's imperative to assert yourself and highlight your company's achievements. However, it would be best to stick to the points that you can prove with data. Otherwise, it could come off as braggadocio and you wouldn't want that.

'Don't give me hubris like, "Oh, I'm gonna be number one in two years,"' Jeffrey Seah speaks from his experience as an investor. 'Show me how, and also, why? Why will the market share give you more money for the same service?'

A region too warm for cold-pitching

Remember Pascal Finette's story of cold-emailing Seth Godin and getting a response within hours? That might not be as easy to pull off in Southeast Asia. As warm as the region may be (literally and figuratively), its people can be a bit conservative in welcoming unfamiliar advances, including cold pitches.

'Asia is one of the places where you definitely really need to just be introduced,' Franco says. 'It is so network based. You need endorsements, you need to know the right people. It's just the way it is for the Philippines, more so likely in Indonesia or Singapore.'

That means, if you have a certain investor in mind and you don't know each other personally, you may have to work through your six degrees of separation to be able to land a meeting.

You can always try cold-pitching, but be aware from the get-go that it could be a hit-or-miss process. To increase the chances of getting noticed, you need to exert a bit more effort.

'Just do the work,' Artie advises. 'Go to LinkedIn, look for a common network, see who your common friends are, ask around and get a semi-warm introduction. That already increases your chances by 100 times.'

SIDEBAR: Penetrating the Inner Circle

From his many years of coaching Southeast Asian family businesses, Prof. Eric Soriano knows that warm introductions are crucial to build a strong network in the region.

'Use family and friends to connect to the investor, because if you're reaching out literally cold, there is always a huge question mark. In Asia, they don't look at the merits, they look at the relationship first. The drawback is, even if the potential investor doesn't like what's going to be pitched, they will agree to the meeting just because, say, the founder is the classmate of their godchild.'

Enrique says the ideal way to get in touch with potential investors would be to have an influential person, a key opinion leader, throw a casual lunch or dinner at home. That person would invite the entrepreneur aiming to raise funds as well as their circle of friends who might be interested to invest. In a region where having an influential backer can give one a significant head start, such a setup is a golden opportunity for founders.

'The key opinion leader is critical because they must have the credibility to back you up and spew good things about you to your target investors.'

But where can you find a key opinion leader who could do this for you? For that, you'll need to tap your current network— former colleagues, fellow alumni, even friends you've met from conventions.

Once you are fortunate enough to have a key opinion leader set up a lunch, don't get overexcited and prop up an iPad to present your pitch deck as guests nibble on appetizers.

'You don't pitch in the house, you socialize. After you get to know them, the pitch will happen somewhere else. It's a matter of getting yourself intimate with the investors, in order to get to know them better. It's a matter of exchanging contact information, giving out calling cards and being invited to their office.'

When you're doing business in another country, getting in touch with your fellow countrymen living in that place certainly helps. And when it comes to making the most out of their network, you can take a cue from the Israelis.

Inbal Arieli, Israeli tech entrepreneur and author of *Chutzpah: Why Israel Is a Hub of Innovation and Entrepreneurship*, tells me about the network of relationships Israelis developed and tap into whenever they need support.

Inbal says that to understand Israelis' strong community network, one must look at two factors. First, Israel is a tiny country of nine million people. That being said, their startups need to address the global market because the local market is just too small.

Second, Israelis have a feeling that they're always a part of a larger movement. In her book, Inbal mentions that in Hebrew, the words 'I' and 'we' come from the same root word.

'You need to find some bridges for the different markets,' Inbal explains. 'We have seen a growing business network of Israelis in Silicon Valley, Europe, Asia, in different places around the world. We have different Israelis living there either for good or for a shorter period of time. And they are always trying to connect and build bridges for the ones that are still here in Israel.'

According to Inbal, Israeli global business networks are efficient. And in a sense, they foster and strengthen Israel as a tech hub.

'You immediately have a landing pad where you can arrive and you immediately have a community of people in the tech ecosystem,' Inbal tells me. 'This is how you get introduced to investors, to new talents, to clients, and it's working really well.'

Language is a factor

Pitching is all about communicating an idea in the best way possible. And in this regard, language is a key factor.

'Southeast Asia is not like the US or Europe that have a very common regulatory framework or a language that people speak. It's very hard to expand in the region here,' Matthijs Geert-Jan van Leeuwen, Sunway iLabs director says. Being a Dutch based in Malaysia, he certainly sees the unique language dynamics in Southeast Asia.

In a region with almost as many official languages and writing systems as there are countries, doing business cross-border can be tricky. For instance, a non-Vietnamese speaker who wants to do business in Vietnam would need to face language barrier difficulties from day one.

'Basically, first are legal concerns,' David Lang says. 'The Vietnamese regulations are basically in Vietnamese, in our native language, and most foreigners find it hard to search online to understand. They come up with different sources of information and they don't know which one is correct.'

Undertaking due diligence in a place where you can't even read store signs can surely be a struggle. But let's dial back a notch and discuss how the language dynamic plays right from the beginning—pitching.

Chris Peralta, who mentors founders, says preparation and iteration are crucial to overcoming the language barrier. And just as your speech teacher used to tell you in school, there's no other way to learn public speaking but to speak in public. Yes, 'practice makes perfect' is an adage we should never take for granted.

Under their incubator-accelerator programme, Chris trains founders, including non-native English speakers to pitch. They've already trained a number of batches from South Korea and he admitted that they had to be tough during training. Every day, each participant had to speak in front of everyone to help develop their articulation and confidence.

'If you're not articulating it properly, people won't understand. And then there's no point in pitching,' Chris says. 'Some of them, we didn't understand when they first pitched. We went through three months. And then at the demo day, we had investors say, "Wow, these startups are amazing." They were able to articulate their whole startup.'

According to Chris, it was the constant practice and getting out of one's comfort zone that allowed the founders to bloom as communicators even if English was not their first language.

Communicating confidently amid cultural expectations

Teaching entrepreneurs how to communicate well is something Jessica Chen does for a living. She is the founder and CEO of Soulcast Media, a strategic business communications agency based in Los Angeles. The Emmy-award winning former news reporter is surely an expert communicator and talking to her now, it's hard to believe that she wasn't as eloquent and confident when she was younger.

An American-born Chinese, Mandarin was Jessica's first language. But more than that, she says cultural expectations were also a factor in her struggle with communication.

'I talk about linking a lot of the cultural elements of why communication was such a struggle for me,' Jessica shares with me. 'And the reason, I've identified myself, are eastern principles: you were taught things of humility, respect, and these are principles that are absolutely so important. But it doesn't necessarily give you that confidence to advocate for yourself, which is so critical at work, or if you're pitching a new idea.'

Despite the culture she was brought up in, Jessica needed to learn how to assert herself. After all, living in the West demanded it of her.

'The culture makes me naturally want to be timider, because I feel like it's better to not rock the boat—don't bother people, don't want to disturb the harmony with anyone,' she admits. 'But because I live in a western society, I always have to remind myself that, wait a second—advocating, communicating, expressing myself is also quite important.'

In the end, it's all about striking the balance between speaking up for oneself without having to show off or boast. After all, no one likes a braggart, and that applies across cultures.

Alongside honing your communication skills, it wouldn't hurt to brush up on various entrepreneurial mindsets and practices around the world. Doing so will enrich your business perspective and gear you to have meaningful conversations with any citizen of the world, when the opportunity presents itself.

Chapter Assignments

Pitching to anyone, anywhere requires honing your communication skills, as well as connecting with different kinds of people on a cultural level. Try these exercises to improve those skills so you can feel more comfortable in doing your pitch in front of a variety of audiences.

- Plant seeds for your long game. Asian networking is all about nurturing connections and maintaining strong relationships. Get in touch with at least three people every week with no other intention but to seek advice.
- Deliver a spontaneous speech every day. Before you start your workday, go on a random question website[5] and answer a random question out loud. This will help you practise organizing your thoughts and expressing them effectively.
- Research what available grants and government support are available in your country. Try to see if you are eligible and try to take advantage of these opportunities. You never know where it could lead as working with the government can open up other resources such as access to the market and opportunities.

---

[5] University of Washington's faculty resource works well: https://faculty.washington.edu/ejslager/random-generator/index.html

Chapter 7: Valuation and Due Diligence

Valuation, as most startup entrepreneurs know, is the process of determining how much a company is valued at—a process that's key for investors, since they need to make calculated judgements about where they will be allocating their funds. While highly focused on the financials of the business, valuation can be seen as a craft—the space between art and science.

In the words of Brian Ngan, Venture Partner at San Francisco-based VU Venture Partners, valuation is a lot like cooking eggs.

It sounds like a far out comparison, but Brian explains: 'The first time you cook eggs, you forget to grease the pan. The next time you do it, you don't let it stick to the pan any more, and you know how to add, say, chives so it tastes better. And then the next time you do it, you do it hotel-grade, adding in a bit of milk. So what we're doing essentially is, we want to be master craftsman of the craft that we choose. And you can only be good at it if you practise it and you do it again and again. You learn from failures and then you get me marginally close to perfection but never quite perfect.'

Valuation, therefore, is part of a startup's due diligence—the examination of your business' financial records—especially when gearing up for a pitch. In this chapter, we will dive into what exactly goes on behind a startup's due diligence process, and how you can arrive at the valuation that works for you.

Due Diligence and the Data Room

So, for a first-time founder, how exactly do you prepare for when an investor needs to conduct their due diligence on your company?

It would be useful, first and foremost, for you to prepare your data room. In *The Final Pitch* Season Four, Podcast Network Asia partners Ron Baetiong and Josef Acuña put the latter's expertise as a capital markets lawyer to good use by preparing all the due diligence documents they knew investors would look for. According to Josef, there are two main things that investors look out for when it comes to due diligence:

- Is there a company to invest in?
- Are there liabilities to look out for?

To address these two concerns, Josef recommends that startups do as they did: first, incorporate, and, second, build a 'data room' or 'deal room'—a database of your confidential corporate documents that investors can simply go through. This could be an actual room or a virtual repository where you can set password restrictions on who can have access, and the goal of the data room is for investors to have visibility on key documents to facilitate due diligence.

In terms of key documents, the data room should contain your:

- Contracts
- Financial Statements
- Capitalization Table
- Employee Information
- Intellectual Property Information

These were all prepared by Josef and Ron during their stint in *The Final Pitch*, specifically their certificate of incorporation and the articles of incorporation, a general info sheet, containing their team's backgrounds and links to their LinkedIn profiles, a table of their current investors and the amount of their investments, and their cap table.

As the data room is expected to contain proprietary information, it's important to be very specific as to who can access this repository. Prepare a list of individuals who can access your data room, and devise a way to monitor who has opened it and when they accessed the documents. It would even be better to grant specific individuals access to certain documents, so you can maintain the confidentiality of your startup's information.

Leticia Souza, vice president of finance at fintech company Uploan.ph, who also has extensive experience in investment banking, says the data room basically verifies that your company is paying taxes, and that your finances are in order. Relevant documents used for sales pitches, onboarding, or a walkthrough of your product are also good to include in that data room.

Outside of that data room, Mark Gorriceta, managing partner of the Gorriceta Africa Cauton & Saavedra law firm, says that part of a startup's due diligence is also doing it on your potential investors. The right questions to ask, he says, are: Is this a VC or an angel? What's their goal? Are you a part of their strategy or does it make sense for their ecosystem to invest in you?

The NDA

A highly important layer of security for your startup is the non-disclosure agreement, or the NDA. Gorriceta likens the NDA to the key to your house; you don't give it to just anyone if they want to do a tour of your home.

'Startups' proprietary information is their most valuable asset. A startup should evaluate the type of documents that it will be sharing, and strategize on when important information will be shared to potential investors. Before sharing proprietary information with third parties (i.e., investors), it is very important that an NDA is entered into by the parties,' advises Mark.

He further adds that standard NDAs should:

- Provide for prohibition against
  - (a) sharing of the confidential/proprietary information to third parties; and
  - (b) using the confidential/proprietary information for personal gain; and
- Identify the documents and information that startups consider as confidential and/or proprietary, and the term of protection.

'Depending on the stage of the negotiation and extent of information to be shared, non-competition and/or non-Solicitation clauses may also be added to an NDA,' adds Gorriceta. 'Ultimately, the special clauses that will need to be included in an NDA will vary on a case-to-case basis.'

The Term Sheet

Aside from the NDA, Gorriceta also identifies these important documents that should also be prepared by startups as part of their due diligence:

- **Non-binding term sheet**. The non-binding term sheet could state exclusivity and confidentiality where, once it is signed, they will do their due diligence for a period of thirty to sixty days. It also includes the commercial terms, for example, that they will place 20 per cent investment in the company.
- **Binding term sheet or binding offer letter.** Otherwise known as the Memorandum of Agreement, this document should have a clause that states 'subject to the terms and conditions of the share purchase agreement, the parties hereby commit as follows', and go on to define more definitive terms of the investment, such as minimum or maximum purchase price. It should also state that the investor will complete its due diligence, and will go to their board with their findings.

If the board thinks the investment is commercially and legally feasible for them, they will now execute a share purchase agreement, and, subject to the terms of that agreement, that would then lead to the sale or acquisition of the company.

Take note that most negotiations will take place once you reach the stage of the share purchase agreement, since this document will include all the terms and milestones of payment.

Arriving at Your Valuation

As part of their due diligence, Josef and Ron also made it a point to prepare a five-year business plan, because their five-year projection served as the justification for the valuation they had for the angel round they raised on *The Final Pitch*.

'Because we were a new company, we didn't have any historical data. We had to show the investors the promise of where we were heading. We felt that the five-year projection was a good indication. I mean, business plans are a story of your company, and we felt that you'll see the whole story if you see the five-year projection,' says Josef.

Circling back to Brian Ngan's description of valuation as a combination of narrative and numbers, Podcast Network Asia's story was that of a growing industry—the business of people *listening* to all these untold stories, on a different platform. 'The story we wanted to tell is that we can coexist with other content platforms; we wanted to project an industry that is thriving and that can actually coexist with other industries that are competing with people's attention,' says Josef.

Josef and Ron's approach to valuation is only one of many, especially for startups that do not have much traction yet. Leticia enumerates three key factors that influence evaluation: the startup's industry, the funding stage they are at, and sometimes, even the season during which they are raising funding.

'That last element might not be so relevant for Asia; I think that is more specific to Silicon Valley, because in the summer, there's nobody there, everybody's on holiday. If you try to raise in September, you may be with a lot of competition,' Leticia explains.

In terms of fundraising stages, Filbert Richerd Ng Tsai, managing director of Equity Labs, a startup-focused professional services firm in the startup sector, shares these methods for each step:

1. Pre-seed and pre-revenue valuation

Filbert recommends that for pre-seed and pre-revenue stages, valuation should focus on TAM SAM SOM: your Total Addressable Market, Serviceable Addressable Market, and Serviceable Obtainable Market. 'The market size that you're considering will be the basis for you to determine the valuation,' he says. 'We basically say, okay, for this type of company, you're targeting this much on the market, for this size of the market, from this much revenue—how much will you be able to generate assuming that a specific number of funding will be injected.'

More specifically, Filbert advises that startups approach this stage of fundraising by looking at these factors:

- Identify how much you are planning to raise. Filbert's example: Your target market is five million subscribers. Assuming you get a $1 million funding, how many of those five million subscribers will you be able to reach with that $1 million?
- Know how much funding you need to achieve a percentage of your potential market—and what you will use the money for. Is it for product development? Marketing? With the marketing budget, how much do you have to spend on ads to reach X number of people?
- For pre-revenue companies, it's best to be very specific: you don't really want your go-to-market strategy to be too big. You don't want to cast too big of a net to capture all the fish, since you won't be able to afford the net.
- You have to know your reach, then your click-through rate, the number of subscribers.

- If you have a free trial for your product, you also have to consider the **churn rate**—the number of people availing the free trial but not subscribing to the product thereafter.

- Aiming for anything higher than 5 per cent of the total market is unreasonable to get, especially when you're a pre-revenue stage company. Filbert's **sample valuation computation for pre-seed stage**: You have a subscription business of $5 per month. In three years, you can achieve 100,000 subscribers. When you achieve that, you have $500,000 recurring revenue per month. In a year, it would be $6 million per year. In the industry for software companies, it would be at 5x, so the valuation is $30 million ($6 million x 5).

To know your market and use that knowledge to arrive at the proper valuation, you need, of course, hard data. For those in the academe, Filbert recommends going through studies by the likes of global market research company Euromonitor, or dataset providers like Statista (you'll have to shell out for the latter). For those who don't have access to those kinds of think tanks, the World Bank is another useful resource, as well as your local statistics authority or agency. The datasets you would need to include are the ones that focus on demographics—total census population, population by age group, gender analysis, gender by age group, potential density per location, and also the population in the major cities.

For fintech startups, specifically, Filbert also recommends reviewing data from your country's central bank, because it is in there that you will find baseline interest rates.

2. Revenue-stage company valuation

According to Brian and Filbert, there are two ways to do valuation for businesses with revenue: the **Discounted Cash Flow (DCF)** or Intrinsic Valuation, and **Relative Valuation**, which is also called the Comparables Approach or Ballpark approach.

'The DCF entails trying to determine the value of the company on its own by looking at how much money it can generate in the next five to ten years. It's the most complex because you have to build a financial model,' says Filbert. 'There are many assumptions in DCF. You need to determine your starting point such as revenue in numbers.'

Here's his example: You're earning $1,000 per month (or go for a non-financial metric: a click-through rate or reach and multiply it by the revenue per subscriber per month). From your revenue in month one, and from there you determine that number. It could be a whole number or percentage. You can also factor in marketing expenses. Example, how much did you spend in month one to come up with that revenue? How much would you need by month two?

To have something to base your assumptions on, Filbert suggests that startups look at:

- Digital marketing analytics (reach, click-through rates, conversions, etc.). This is especially useful for business-to-consumer (B2C) tech startups.
- Data from traffic or the number of people passing through your location (for retail startups); marketing for fintech startups.
- For business-to-business (B2B), the number of leads that your business development team can actually generate per month.

Table 1: Sample DCF Computation

	Revenue	Cost	Profit (=Revenue-Cost)
Year 1	$1,200,000	$4,000,000	−$2,800,000
Year 2	$2,400,000	$4,000,000	−$1,600,000
Year 3	$3,600,000	$4,000,000	−$400,000
Year 4	$4,800,000	$4,000,000	+$800,000
Year 5	$6,000,000	$4,000,000	+$2,000,000
TOTAL			−$2,000,000
Year 6			$2,000,000 / 0.25 = $8,000,00
Total			$6,000,000

For Relative Valuation, or the Comparables Approach or Ballpark approach, this entails comparing the company to another company in almost a totally same stage. 'If Company X is only ahead of Company Y by one month, and Company X is valued at $10 million, you can also assume that Company Y is valued the same,' says Filbert. 'However, if it is between different industries, then you can't do that because it won't make sense; it should be very similar in business model and stage of the business.'

Moreover, Filbert recommends that startups working on their valuation compare themselves to someone publicly available, and make adjustments to it. You need to understand your business—and then find whatever is closest to your business.

3. The mindset of valuation: Is higher better?

Beyond the numbers and the narrative, what Filbert calls 'the mindset of doing valuation'—what drives value—is what he believes startups truly need to learn when raising funds.

'At the end of the day, for a lot of startups, valuation is not really mathematical at all; it is not really as systematic. When it comes to your investors, they will judge how good you are at executing your business, because at the end of the day they can just infuse their money into another company that is doing something similar to you and they can just manage the business, or actually they can just do a whole new business unit within their company and run it as their own,' Filbert explains. 'So what's important for these startup founders is to really identify what drives the value of their company. Identify those qualitative factors that investors would be looking at rather than squarely focusing on the mathematical aspect, or trying to find a way to push your valuation to $20 million.'

The problem with aiming for the highest valuation, at least in the seed round, is that it could put off future investors, especially if the startup does not grow so much after that initial funding. 'The only thing a high valuation does is limit the amount of equity that you have to give up, which is another problem,' explains Patrick Gentry of Sprout Solutions. 'Understand that if you're going the VC route, you're going to give up a ton of equity to get capital and grow this business to its maximum potential.'

Steve Sy, founder of Philippines-based e-commerce enabler Great Deals, pretty much says the same thing: that higher isn't necessarily better when it comes to valuation.

He had the enviable dilemma of having a good number of investors who wanted to invest in his company, and had to choose which one was the best fit. Instead of going for the highest valuation for their Series B funding, they instead chose one that could give them more strategic value. As Steve says, 'Sometimes it's not just about money.'

They ended up with the Fast Logistics Group, which invested, together with global private equity firm CVC Capital Partners, $30 million for Great Deals' Series B funding. With Great Deals aiming to improve the logistics aspect of the e-commerce industry (Steve's goal is to create 'micro' warehouses to enable faster delivery to consumers); this was definitely a more strategic route for Steve and his company.

SIDEBAR: Something to Consider: Bridge Rounds

A bridge round, as the term suggests, is something startups can explore when they are in between their Series funding rounds. Amra Naidoo of Accelerating Asia says this is not usually top of mind for startups, but it is a process that could help them potentially manage their valuation.

'A bridge round is really good because it's often a smaller round. It's quicker to raise, so typically, you raise between $300,000 to $800,000 depending on the business model and where the investors are coming from as well,' says Amra. 'Within three months typically, 100 per cent of our startups would close both rounds during that time, so it's a lot more capital-efficient and time-efficient than going out and trying to raise, you know, a gigantic Series A, which many have aspirations to do. The other thing is that the bridge round helps them actually get to a level where they can go and talk to institutional investors. Often, Series A can take a year to raise. A bridge round allows them to raise quicker and establish relationships.'

Chapter Assignments

Doing your due diligence, which includes arriving at the valuation that best suits your company, is integral to the startup journey. Perform these exercises as a team so you are sure to cover all your bases when it comes to taking stock of your company's financial data.

- Meet with your team and start collating all your documents for your virtual data room.
- As a team, determine the valuation method most suitable to your startup and start working through the numbers to determine the valuation that best works for you.
- Solicit the opinion of other startups and finance professionals who have gone through the process of valuation of their or other companies.

Act 3: The Journey Onwards

Chapter 8: Insights from Around the World

'Experience is a master teacher, even when it's not our own.'

—Gina Greenlee

Throughout the book, I've shared with you bits and pieces of advice from the startup experts that I have had the fortune of meeting or working with. In this chapter, I'm sharing with you more nuggets of wisdom I've received from some of the world's best startup and innovation ecosystems, thought leaders, and visionaries—in their own words. These are the lessons that they learnt from decades of experience, hard work, failures and triumphs. Think of these snippets as candy for the brain, hacks to learning a ton of valuable insights into pitching, business, innovation, resilience and life in general, compressed in one loaded chapter.

Tim Draper

Founder of Draper Associates and Draper University

San Mateo, CA—It took a few minutes for Jonathan Jaranilla to arrive, but he eventually crossed over from an adjacent building towards Draper University, the Silicon Valley startup incubator campus of third-generation venture capitalist Tim Draper. It was a Saturday morning and my wife, Monica, and I just got off our Uber ride lugging around our suitcases, as this was our next stop before heading to San Francisco City.

His company Ledger Atlas was one of Tim's portfolio companies, and Jonathan, together with his co-founder Matt Kolling, were old friends from Manila. Jonathan promised a tour of Hero City, Draper University's co-working facilities, next time we were in Silicon Valley, and we were happy to take him up on his offer.

Stepping into Hero City is like entering Disneyland for startups. The first thing that greets you is the reception counter made out of a Tesla 3. As one of the early investors of Tesla, the Tesla reception counter is a literal symbol of where Tim puts his money. In big bold caricatures, you will see superheroes donning the walls of the large expanse.

We never got a chance to meet face-to-face during my visit, but for this book, Tim Draper gladly gave his advice to budding startups.

John Aguilar (JA): What would be your advice to a startup from the east (particularly Southeast Asia) who would like to pitch to you or other investors from Silicon Valley?

Tim Draper (TD): It is important to use your current country to test your product in, but once you have the customer product fit, you should be thinking globally. Make sure your product or service is the best in the world, not just the best in your region. Also, I recommend thinking long and hard about the business model and how you are going to delight your customer.

JA: You always ask your students to think global when they plan. How far down the road should a startup communicate its vision for world domination without coming off as too ambitious or unrealistic?

TD: I don't think there is a limit. More ambitious is always better. Go for world domination—and do it in the market, not by trying to control a bunch of people politically.

JA: What's it like working with Elon Musk and what is it about his manner of thinking and engaging with people that makes you believe that he will succeed in whatever he says he will set out to do? Is there a trait you find in him that you also find in other successful startup founders?

TD: Confidence is big. So is a willingness to go after the biggest problems and the biggest opportunities. Elon said, 'We're going to Mars.' That made me realize that whether he got there or not, he would get the best engineers, and something great would come of it.

JA: Any insights you can share with us on founders pitching to you on *Meet the Drapers*? Is a pitch done on a TV show different than say one that's done without any cameras rolling?

TD: If you can get on *Meet the Drapers*, do it. Companies who get to pitch are reaching twelve million potential customers now, as well as twelve million potential investors. If you are chosen to be on the show, I recommend rehearsing over and over, and be ready for any questions we might throw at you.

JA: If you could tell any founder the one thing they should not do when they pitch to you, what would that be?

TD: Don't oversell. So many people are always selling to VCs. It becomes overwhelming. Best to just lay out your vision, your product, how it works, and your business plan and business model and then get ready for questions.

Patrick Grove

Australian serial internet and media entrepreneur

The first time I had any knowledge of Patrick Grove was during my preliminary research on *Shark Tank*-esque formats for *The Final Pitch*. Patrick was one of the investors for *Angel's Gate*, a Singapore-based reality pitching series where he, along with a few investors, heard pitches in an all-white set that resembled heaven. Yes, they were dressed in all-white ensembles as well so go figure. I met him for the first time during a startup event in Manila, and have been connected online since then.

He's come a long way since those days of hearing pitches from the pearly gates, and as the co-founder and CEO of Catcha Group, the man has an ever-growing list of new companies, acquisitions and IPOs we can all learn from

John Aguilar (JA): From the outside looking in, it seems like raising money now and getting people to believe in a new venture you put together is so easy because of your reputation and track record. Before all of this, how in your early years did you manage to pitch your vision to people (whether it's for funding or joining you at Catcha/ iProperty)? How has this changed through the years?

Patrick Grove (PG): Nothing has changed and it isn't easier. Every venture is just as hard as every other venture for funding. For our SPAC, we did close to fifty meetings. For the company before that, we averaged about a 100 meetings. Fundraising is never easy! It's just a matter of time before you find someone that shares your vision and is willing to commit if you persevere.

JA: As an investor, what do you look for in a startup/founder that is non-negotiable? Are there any specific traits that resonate with you and that you look for?

PG: Hunger and perseverance. Just those two really. If you have that, 90 per cent of the battle is over.

JA: What is the best pitch you've ever done and what makes it so memorable?

PG: Oftentimes the ones where I get a no, and the person gives me honest feedback as to why it's a no. I love learning from every interaction.

JA: Entrepreneurs have pitched to you in the reality TV series *Angel's Gate*. What would be your advice for people pitching on a reality TV show?

PG: Know your stuff and your numbers!

Inbal Arieli

Author, serial entrepreneur, and business executive

When they found out I was writing a book called *The Art and Science of the Pitch*, the embassy of Israel in Manila sent me a couple of books—among them, *Start-Up Nation: The Story of Israel's Economic Miracle* by Dan Senor and Saul Singer, and a copy of author Inbal Arieli's book called *Chutzpah: Why Israel is a Hub for Innovation and Entrepreneurship*. I initially thought of Chutzpah as a business book, but as I turned the pages, I also realized that it's also a parenting book, owing to her thesis that the entrepreneurial mindset of Israelis was fostered through their unorthodox parenting style.

Inbal fostered her entrepreneurial skills during her mandatory military service as a lieutenant in the Israel Defence Forces (IDF) elite intelligence 8,200 unit. After completing her service and for the past twenty plus years, she held leading roles in the flourishing Israeli tech sector. She lectures widely to business and government leaders around the world, analysing and discussing the most critical leadership skills, based on how Israeli culture breeds risk taking and entrepreneurship at a very young age.

When I interviewed Inbal for my podcast, *Methods to Greatness*, in May 2021, there was an outbreak of violence in the Israeli–Palestinian conflict. Before we recorded, Inbal warned me and my production staff not to panic if we hear sirens, alarms or rockets in the background. This only goes to show Inbal's professionalism and work ethic as an individual even during uncertain times.

John Aguilar (JA): I am very interested in how you wrote in your book that Israel, or should I say, the concept of Israel having the highest percentage of startups per capita worldwide, is largely attributed to the IDF.

Inbal Arieli (IA): At the age of eighteen, most Israelis join the military, men and women, and the screening process starts before, around the age of sixteen and a half. At that age, you don't really understand, and maybe lastly but most importantly, you lack the relevant experience. That actually means that you are not focusing on what you already know, or what you think you know— your past experience. You are actually focusing on your potential and what you could learn and what you could turn into and that opens an entire new world of opportunities, both for the candidates and for the military.

JA: You also make a case of this mindset actually not being born in the military but way back—on the way you approach every day as kids, and a great example that you gave in your book is the typical Israeli playground.

IA: I really think that this innovative, resilient, accountable mindset does not come at the age of eighteen, as a magical moment. The involvement, development—that happens throughout our childhood. Our soft skills muscles are truly trained from a very young age. The typical Israeli playground just lets kids play in a free environment without too much guidance. You will see Israeli kids at the young age of two to four just doing whatever they want. A lot of noise, jumping all over, bumping into each other, yes, but they figure it out by themselves. And they confront these small conflicts, they learn how to resolve them, and there's an entirely different rhythm and tempo to an Israeli playground. To me, the roots of creativity and risk-taking, management, teamwork, and coping with uncertainty, that's where it starts.

JA: A lot of cultures adopted giving everyone a medal for joining a race. Everyone's a winner, but in reality, what does that do with everyone's competitiveness, one's ability to also accept defeat and say, *I did not do well, I have to work harder?*

IA: Without being capable of looking into failures right in the eyes and understanding that these were mistakes, we can't learn from them. So, I think that it is about finding your inner motivation. In all these contests and external motivation that you get, it's the world giving feedback to you. When I talk to young entrepreneurs, I tell them to always be open to external feedback. I'm not afraid to say that I've failed in some activities or startups. It doesn't mean I'm a failure. It means that I made wrong decisions, bad choices, or had not learnt quick enough and corrected.

JA: When it comes to pitching, is there anything we can learn from Israelis in terms of how they think about things and pitch?

IA: When you work with a US-based startup accelerator, there would be very clear best practices, guidelines and structures that actually work on creating the right pitch. And it works. What does not work there is adapting that pitch with nuances and the person in part. And I think that is what works for Israelis in their chaotic *balagan*[6] pitches—because of the fact that they don't put too much emphasis on the structure, and you know, having a clear narrative one-size-fits-all pitch. What they do is, they come into a conversation. And so, their pitch would sound differently to an investor versus a tech-savvy client. It can be more easily adapted to the person, to the human being in front of them and that actually is the important element in pitching.

Insights from Silicon Valley

No study of technology and tech culture would be complete without an exploration of its mecca, Silicon Valley. I would like to share some of my most interesting takeaways from my trips to Silicon Valley—trips that I have taken as part of R&D as well as personal and entrepreneurial growth. Some are lessons that are quite controversial, while some validate things we were already thinking of implementing in our own businesses.

Insight # 1 from AWS: The Amazon Press Release

Employees are not allowed to use PowerPoints when pitching a new idea within Amazon. The reason for this? When you have to write prose in complete sentences, it forces you to think through in more detail the ideas you are presenting. By not using PowerPoints, they also remove the effect of charm, personality, and leadership that some people have when they present, which forces people to concentrate more on the ideas. The unorthodox mechanism by which a new idea is proposed at Amazon is an internal press release. It's essentially a visionary document that is written like it would go out to the press, but given at the start of an idea presentation meeting. The press release is written in such a way that it makes one think of the new product or service as

---

[6] *Balagan* is a Russian-derived Hebrew word for chaos, mess, or disarray.

though it were already out, forcing the proponents of the idea to be in the shoes of the customer. It would even have quotes from 'satisfied customers'. In addition to the press release, there is a set of questions, between three to six pages, depending on what analysts, press or customers would ask to clarify some of the points in the press release. These are all the questions that need to be asked and answered to identify precisely who is the customer? What exactly is the opportunity? What is the benefit to the customer? All of this is done even before a single line of code is written.

Insight # 2 from Salesforce: Ohana Culture

One of the biggest reasons why people join and stay in an organization is due to its culture. If you are pitching your company to your potential team members and partners, you might want to take a page from how the culture was born at Salesforce. When Salesforce CEO Marc Benioff decided to take a sabbatical in the late '90s in Hawaii, he connected with locals and learnt many of Hawaii's traditions and customs, among them the concept of Ohana. In Hawaiian culture, Ohana represents the idea that families—blood related, adopted, or intentional—are bound together, and that families are responsible for one another. Marc made sure this was part of Salesforce culture when he later established the company. When I visited the Salesforce HQ on Mission Street in San Francisco, we were toured by a tight-knit Filipino community that calls itself the Filipino Ohana, their employee resource group for Filipinos. We immediately felt right at home and had a sense that the Filipino employees of Salesforce were very well represented and supported, having a more intimate family within the bigger Salesforce organization. Their Ohana culture has earned them recognition around the world, bagging award for 'world's best workplace' and 'most innovative company', just to name a few. They also have the 1-1-1 Philanthropic Model, which dedicates 1 per cent of the company's equity, 1 per cent of its product, and 1 per cent of employees' time back to the community.

When your company allots time off for you to give 1 per cent of your paid company time to volunteer for the community, you know you're part of something special.

Insight # 3 from Google: 20 per cent Project

One of the legendary examples of innovation culture in Silicon Valley is Google's 20 per cent time or 20 per cent project. An astounding 20 per cent of Google employees' time is given to them to encourage working on 'projects' for Google that may or may not be outside their traditional role. Imagine being able to work on anything you want to do that can even be outside your core function in the company. These projects have been so successful that Gmail and Google Maps actually began as side projects that eventually morphed into what they are today. Of course, it does help that Google's perks allow their employees to practically live on the Google campus or Googleplex, as they provide everything including all meals, something that I got to personally experience. But that's another story.

Insights from Singapore

From the West and the Middle East, let's move on to a place a little closer to my home, right here in Southeast Asia. Singapore didn't use to be the startup hotbed it is today. In 2000, a study by the Global Entrepreneurship Monitor suggested that only 2.1 per cent of Singapore's population was involved in starting or running their own business.

Members of the Parliament attributed the sluggish entrepreneurial growth rate to a phenomenon called 'No U-Turn Syndrome' or NUTS. This term, coined by Creative Technology co-founder Sim Wong Hoo, describes Singaporeans' mindset of fearing any action without higher authorities' permission. Singaporean drivers, for instance, will not make a U-turn if there's no U-turn sign.

To encourage entrepreneurship and expose young people to business, the National University of Singapore launched NUS

Overseas Colleges (NOC) programme in 2001, which sent students to entrepreneurial hubs around the globe, including Silicon Valley. After all, there weren't any role models or mentors in the city-state at that time, and Singaporeans had to venture elsewhere to learn and hone their entrepreneurial skills. It was an experiment that raked in good returns and produced more than 800 startups by students and alumni.

Today, the country is home to 55,000 startups, ranging from deep tech and e-commerce to fintech, according to the Singapore Economic Development Board. Bloomberg ranked Singapore as the sixth-most innovative city in the world and the top in Asia Pacific.

To cater to the growing number of startups, NUS Enterprise, Singtel Innov8 and the then Media Development Authority of Singapore collaborated in 2011 to turn an industrial building up for demolition into a startup hub, offering cheap office rent to founders trying to get their company off the ground. That innovation hub is BLOCK 71, named after its address in Ayer Rajah industrial estate.

My pilgrimage visit to Block 71 was as a side trip when I attended the Singapore Fintech Festival (SFF) 2019, and the Singapore Week of Innovation and Technology (SWITCH), which drew over 45,000 participants from 140 countries. As there were many side events, I made sure to attend one event at Block 71 organized by NUS Enterprise in partnership with Singtel Innov8.

Before the actual event, I made sure to walk around Block 71 first just to get a feel of the place. Walking around, I saw a plethora of startup offices, and within those offices rows and rows of workstations, similar in vibe and feel to the ones that I've seen in Silicon Valley. Inside the venue for the community event, there was a steady, casual vibe. There were the event sponsors—Kris Lab, Singapore Airlines' digital innovation lab, and ecosystem players. Local Singapore startup founders were interspersed with attendees of different nationalities, perhaps a mix of ecosystem players, and visitors such as me attending the SFF.

Over a few beers, I managed to talk to a number of startups who told me how Block 71 was a very convenient way to build a product because of the existing network of people who are literally your officemates in the same building. 'If you want users to test something or you need to validate an idea, you just ping some of your friends to come over and you can easily get their feedback for a new product or feature you're working on,' one said to me.

Block 71, at over a thousand startups in the neighbourhood, probably has the most concentrated and dense startup ecosystem in the world. Singapore has cracked the code and has given startups a vibrant and tight startup playground ecosystem in this Garden City. This is something to think about and probably emulate in the different startup ecosystems around the world.

Sinigang Valley

In Manila, the beginnings of something similar are now slowly taking shape. Sinigang Valley located in the hip neighbourhood of Poblacion in the fringes of Manila's financial capital Makati, is a collective of startups, VC funds, and ecosystem players that decided that it was about time to create our own version of a tech and innovation epicentre.

Sinigang is a Filipino soup made with meat, shrimp or fish, vegetables, and flavoured with a sour ingredient such as tamarind or guava. It's a mix of ingredients and can be considered a complete meal by itself, a fitting description for the eclectic, creative vibe espoused by the community.

Franco Varona, Managing Partner at Foxmont Capital Partners and one of the proponents of the Sinigang Valley Association, tells me how he and a bunch of successful startup founders, restaurant and bar owners, and startup ecosystem enablers, decided to band together to form Sinigang Valley. I wanted to check things out, but as we were deep in lockdown as of this book's writing, the Omicron Covid-19 variant has made congregation in groups of any size an impossible proposition.

We discuss the possibility of my own startup venture builder and co-working facility Dragon's Nest, located in Quezon City in the north, becoming an extension of Sinigang Valley. We opened up Dragon's Nest to be a venture builder of startups that we would be building in the Philippines but whose primary objective would be to be able to scale across the Southeast Asian region. We agree to have co-located events to strengthen the startup ecosystem in a much more focused, concerted effort, and we would do it as soon as physically possible.

There are many more independent initiatives—from the government and the private sector—strewn across the different regions of the country, all trying to see how they can contribute as startup enablers in the Philippines. QBO, Ideaspace, Startup Village, Spring Valley, the Philippine Chamber of Commerce and industry (PCCI)-Innovation Centre, the Technology Incubation Programme (TBI) of the Department of Science and Technology (DOST), and so many more.

The Philippines, after waiting for so long, is now on the cusp of finally realizing its potential as a startup hotspot in Asia. Not only are we blessed with an English-speaking workforce, but we have now entered our demographic sweet spot, the state where the country's working-age population is relatively larger than its dependents (those who are too young or too old to work). The growing internet penetration, influx of affordable smartphones, and the pandemic—which forced many industries towards a rapid digitization—has made it possible for a number of our technology startups and conglomerates' technology arms to grow exponentially their user base, influence and, consequently, their valuation. This has enabled local tech companies to raise money from big foreign funds, which previously did not even consider the Philippines on their investment radar.

Things are looking up for Philippine tech and our startups. And if there's anything I have learnt from my travels to different tech ecosystems and from talking to those who have built their own, it's the acceptance that you can never completely replicate the success of Silicon Valley, as each place is unique and will have different nuances, communities and markets, and like water, each will find its own unique path towards success.

Chapter 9: Lights, Camera, Action!

'Steal like an artist.'

—Austin Kleon

After learning the essentials of pitching and gaining insights from some of the world's best, perhaps you're excited to get the show on the road. One of the paths you may want to take is pitching on a reality show.

Yes, a reality show gives you a chance to get funded, but more than that, it provides an opportunity to learn from mentors you otherwise may not have the privilege to work with. Most of all, it will give you exposure—something of great value when you want to get your brand in front of customers, potential team members and, hopefully, more investors.

As the showrunner of *The Final Pitch* for several seasons now, and as a long-time TV producer in the reality genre, I've compiled a few helpful resources for anyone who wants to audition for and participate in a reality TV competition.

How to Nail an Audition for a Reality TV Show

If there is anyone who can give a masterclass on how to audition for a reality TV show, it would be *The Amazing Race Asia* Season Two contestants Rovilson Fernandez and Marc Nelson. Rovilson and I go way back, from the time when people still sat in front of the TV to watch shows together. When I interviewed him on my podcast *Methods to Greatness*, I asked him about how they auditioned for the adventure reality game show franchise.

'That was super premeditated, bro,' Rovilson told me. 'Because in all honesty, the real race is the auditions, not through *The Amazing Race* itself, you're only going against eleven other teams. In the audition process, you're going up against thousands of teams. So you have to make yourself stand out there.'

Since both of them were already TV hosts, Rovilson and Marc took advantage of their resources and put together a kick-ass audition tape. From professional makeup artists and photographers to directors and sound designers, they made the most out of their contacts and left nothing to chance.

'We had a script, I wrote it. It was inspired by the Apple commercial at the time. It was, "I'm a PC. I'm a Mac", and we were just showing our differences,' Rovilson recalled. 'It's one of my finest pieces of work.'

If you're curious on how these guys made their audition tape, search it up online and you'll see an awesome study on making an impact when you're trying to get into a reality show.

'Michael McKay, the producer of *The Amazing Race Asia*, pulled us aside one day and he said "Your audition tape was the best I've ever seen", and, you know, coming from him, we were just, like, wow,' Rovilson shared. 'That just made us realize that if you do your research, put your work in, put your time in, you will get great returns.'

How to Prepare and Audition for a Reality Pitching Show

Whether it's *The Final Pitch*, *Shark Tank*, or *Dragon's Den*, it takes a certain level of preparation to make it and do well. Here's straight up advice if you are looking to land a deal or make an impact with your participation on a made-for-TV pitching competition:

- Invest time and effort into your audition video. Oftentimes, producers will cast you for the show just on the merit of what they see on your pitch video. For *The Final Pitch*, you don't have to put on a show because making it on the show is based on the merit of your business and not so much on the way you project on camera. But I would be lying to you if I didn't say that the impact you make on that video pitch goes a long way. A submission video is meant for the producers to see you and your personality, so never submit a collage of you or your slide deck edited to music because first and foremost, we want to see you speak and see how you project on camera.

- Research the investors. This is one of the most important things you can do because you have to know what makes them tick and what they would most likely find an interest in. It's even likely that you would know who you and your business are most likely most compatible with.

- Make your story relatable. Producers are looking to put someone on TV with something that people can relate to. If what you are pitching is something that is very industry specific or highly niche, find an anecdote or experience that people can relate to so you can bring the story of the product to life.

- Know and give your ask. In the audition process, I cannot count the number of times that the entrepreneur pitches without actually giving an ask. More than a lack of foresight, it shows an utter lack of preparation. If you come into a pitch competition, you are there not just to look cute but to actually ask for something. Make sure that what you are asking for is clear to you and the audience, as it is the main reason you're there to begin with.

- Know your numbers. Sometimes this can be the make or break so be ready with all your finances and be prepared to get on a call with someone you can consult with in the event you need advice or approval for a high-stakes decision.

- Look good. Believe me, this helps a lot. There is nothing wrong with jeans and your startup logo-emblazoned shirt but if you can, throw in a blazer and make sure you comb your hair. You putting some effort into the way you look shows your respect for the investors and the audience watching the show.

- Your slides are there to merely support you. Don't make it the centre of attention. And please, don't use it as a teleprompter! Words should be in white and your background must be dark or black so that the camera can pick up the words.

- Have the track record to back yourself up. There is nothing more enticing than listening to someone who has built great things in the past. If you have done great things, let the judges know about it. It will only make what you are pitching all the more interesting if they know that the one pitching has done well.

- Have an excellent online presence. The investors and their teams will Google you, as will everyone in the future who sees your pitch and takes an interest in you. And that includes the potential customers and investors who will see your pitch on TV or online in the future.

- Practise, practise, practise. There is no substitute for this and never just wing your pitch. You'll know when a pitch is practised or if someone is just winging it when the person is trying to grasp the right words or is unsure how to transition from one part of the pitch to the next.

My final piece of advice for anyone who wants to be part of a reality pitching show is to do it for the right reasons. There are many upsides to putting yourself out there, but never do it just for the sake of getting attention without actually wanting to get a deal done. The producers and the investors will most likely see through you if your intention is merely to get an additional marketing push, and it just really leaves a bad taste in the mouth.

All things considered, pitching on a reality pitching show is like the perfect storm. If you get the funding, TV exposure and long-term goodwill from having projected yourself well, there is no reason this cannot be your ticket to bigger things.

Startup Fitscovery getting the investor judges' hearts pumping with a live demo

(L-R) Investor judge Mikee Romero, William Tiu Lim, John Aguilar, Michael Dargani, and Mark Vernon

John guests on CNN Philippines' *The Final Word* with Rico Hizon

Ceremonial toast to end the season

John with wife and business partner, Monica

Chapter 10: Conclusion

'Never let the future disturb you. You will meet it, if you have to, with the same weapons of reason which today arms you against the present.'

—Marcus Aurelius

As I've said in the first few pages of this book, one of the reasons I wrote it is to prepare myself to make some of the biggest pitches in my life so far. I've used this book both as a journal as well as a way to reach out to the best minds who can also help me craft and hone my pitch. I've helped hundreds of entrepreneurs pitch their businesses on our show, and I've also just finished writing the book *The Art and Science of the Pitch*.

It's now time to use this book to help me pitch *The Final Pitch*.

My first pitches will be to strategic investors in the Philippines who would be able to help us expand our reach even further. The next round would be for our regional expansion to onboard partners and investors who would be our partners in Singapore, Malaysia, Indonesia, Thailand and Vietnam.

The following pages were written in one day—the day of my deadline to submit this book. Some of it is my mind meandering on different thoughts as I vacillate on the pros and cons of my planned moves. I've used the chapters as a checklist and windshield wipers to see if what I wrote will cover all the bases.

Here we go.

17 January 2022—Day of manuscript deadline.

If I go through the book that I've just written, what particular points do I apply? In the next few pages, I'll outline all of those relevant to my pitch, and put everything into action. This *should* work.

Chapter 1: The Entrepreneurial Journey

If I look at myself and my journey as an entrepreneur so far, what does this tell me about where I would like to go? As a TV producer, I've had glorious failures but I've also had big wins. *The Final Pitch* is without a doubt the most important show we've produced to date.

Producing *The Final Pitch* has been one of the most fulfilling endeavours of my life. To imagine it out of nothing and to see all these founders now build upon the break and funding they were given through the show gives me and my team immense satisfaction. It's been a source of pride and joy as we are able to help so many people.

On the business side, *The Final Pitch* as well as my other shows and businesses are what may be called 'lifestyle businesses', and have allowed me to feed my family, build our beautiful home, and live the lifestyle we have become accustomed to. But for it to evolve into a 'growth business', I know that I would need to involve more people and fuel to see this rocket ship take flight. One thing I know for sure. I'm on a ten-year sprint to build a multi-million-dollar group of companies.

Chapter 2: Knowing Your 'Why' and Finding Your 'Who'

Knowing your 'Why'

After I graduated from college, I wrote down a bucket list of things I would like to accomplish in my life and put it in my wallet. As the years progressed, I was able to cross out entries one-by-one.

Twenty years later, I realized that I had crossed out every single entry on the list. And so, I made a new one.

I looked at the old list to reflect on the things that I wanted to do as a young man at the time, and tried to dig deep into what I wanted to do next. The new list is an improvement or next step from my old list in my 20s. I also decided that I want to be able to cross out all the items off the list in ten years.

Two entries are particularly relevant for this chapter:

- Help scale 1,000 entrepreneurs and startups.
- Build a billion-peso business.

The former was born from our company mission and vision, and is a direct manifestation of my 'why':

'To provide opportunities for entrepreneurs and startups to be nation builders.'

The latter, from something I always tell my seven-year-old son before I tuck him into bed every night.

'Sweet big dreams.'

Finding your 'Who'

In my twenties, I wanted to become an entrepreneur. I wanted the freedom to do my own thing, to freely pursue my passions, and to not be answerable to anyone but myself.

I always used to want to be in full control, but as I've matured as an entrepreneur I've slowly got that out of my system, and my perspective has changed. I often think of the African proverb, 'If you want to go fast, go alone. If you want to go far, go together.' In order for me to go far, I must work with other people, collaborate with them, work towards a common, bigger objective, and plan for the end game for the future. If before I was so protective of my independence and autonomy, I am now at a point where I am seeking others' opinions, knowledge and resources.

We need to now involve the most strategic partners that can help us turn *The Final Pitch* into a multi-million-dollar global media empire.

For us to grow, I need to understand the minds of investors more intimately, so I would need venture capitalists on my side. More than an investor, the VCs would also serve as mentors and help me think through the deals that can be structured in the future.

The first person who comes to mind is Franco Varona, managing partner of Foxmont Capital Partners. We had only met online when I reached out to him one time on LinkedIn months into the pandemic. What struck me with Franco was his desire to help Filipino and Philippine-focused startups. His fund's initial investments into local media tech companies were good indicators that he had a nose for successful media properties. I told Franco that we would eventually be raising to fund the expansion of *The Final Pitch* across Southeast Asia, and that I would most likely pitch to him and another investor, Singapore-based Jeffrey Seah, partner at Quest Ventures.

After hearing our business model, Franco graciously gave advice on how we could increase the valuation of our company. I took this as a positive sign, as he was essentially giving me advice on how we could increase the value of our company, instead of downplaying its value—a company that his fund could potentially invest in, in the future.

I may not have pitched anything to Franco that time, but I knew then that I wanted him on my team.

Chapter 3: What Are They Thinking?

Knowing your audience

After Christmas of 2021, I finally invite Franco to Dragon's Nest, our beautifully appointed HQ, which unfortunately has been closed for the past two years during the pandemic. I wanted him to see our place of business, our plans for expansion, the look and feel of the place. It was as much a part of my pitch as it was what was on my deck.

'We're seeking $1million for a 20 per cent stake in *The Final Pitch Philippines*,' I said when I came to the 'Ask' slide. 'After that, we'll raise again for our regional expansion.'

I wanted to gauge Franco's reaction to my pitch and our ask. But more than that, I wanted to get to know Franco some more.

After the meeting, I invited him to have lunch at my house. This is where I got to know him more as a person. It was during the lunch that he told me about how he once wrote a letter in 2001 to his mother, talking about how he promised her that he would come back to the Philippines and make a difference. This story made me realize that we share the same desire to help our country, and we were kindred spirits. If we share the same mission, together, I felt we could go a long way.

'But at the end of the day,' Franco concluded, 'as a VC, I need to see the exit.'

That makes my ask almost irrelevant. The vision is clear. But the exit strategy, that is what I have to really prepare for.

Chapter 4: The Elements of a Pitch

So what was in my slide deck? I've outlined below the contents of my short-form pitch to Franco:

- The Opportunity
  The Final Pitch has helped hundreds of entrepreneurs and startups in the Philippines. However, we could help so many more, and create a bigger impact—in the Philippines and beyond.
- The Solution
  Involve the bigger media companies and co-produce the show with them.
- The Ask
  $1 million for 20 per cent equity stake in *The Final Pitch* Philippines.
- Minimum Viable Product (MVP)
  Through our seven seasons on-air, we have helped over a hundred startups and funded millions of dollars into the startup ecosystem. We've been profitable since day one.
- The Team
  We have a solid team of veterans and young creatives, and a scalable system driven by people who believe in the show's vision.

- Business Model
  The investor judges are invited to be co-producers of each season of *The Final Pitch*. We get a success fee from investments made through the show.
- Market Analysis
  We are the first and only business reality show in the Philippines. The potential to scale across Southeast Asia is huge.
- Milestones/Future Plans
  Q2, 2022: We produce our upcoming eighth season, 'Tech Edition' on CNN Philippines.
  Q1, 2023: We produce *The Final Pitch ASEAN*.
- Financial Projections
  We show them the profitability of the show and potential for future seasons, and why they should be part of it.

Chapter 5: Pitching Style and Technique

I've got a solid pitch deck and have committed my pitch to my head. But I know I still have to look, sound, and feel good during the days of my pitches. Most days, I always just make sure that I rest and eat well and exercise to make sure that I'm ready to give a great pitch.

Except for Franco whom I pitched to in person, I'll be pitching to others in the near future online. Depending on who I'm pitching to, I adjust my top accordingly. If I'm pitching to a young VC, I will wear any of my ten black collared shirts. If I'm pitching to a corporate, I will wear a long-sleeved polo shirt. Unless I am moderating an event or guesting on CNN Philippines, I never put on a blazer for a presentation as it seems too pretentious given the fact that the other person knows I'm just at home—in tropical Philippines.

I have two backgrounds. One is that of my home office, which has books neatly stacked in shelves behind me, and another is a wall of our bedroom, nice and clean white background with a beautiful black-and-white painting by one of my favourite artists, Ombok Villamor. Depending on my mood or who I have a meeting with, I would choose any of the two. The home office background is usually for work meetings, and the bedroom background is for when I am making a presentation and I want to make an impression. The impression I want to make is that I am clear-minded and focused, I have good taste, and I have flair.

In both setups I have adequate three-point lighting, and make sure that if I am making a pitch, I will lock the door so no one comes in.

I open with a smile and very brief chit-chat, and thank them for getting on the call with me.

Before I begin my pitch, I try to ask something about them that would help me frame and contextualize my pitch. Perhaps it's something I read about them or their company that I would like to get clarity on. Since I've initiated the call and announced that I'll be presenting my slides, I go ahead and ask them ever so casually before I proceed about how their business or investments are doing now, or even their investment thesis if I am unsure. Them talking about this to me at the onset gives me the information I need, and allows them to trust me, knowing that I am aware of where they are at.

I begin my presentation with the opening billboard of *The Final Pitch*, which usually almost always elicits a positive response. I then deliver my pitch with a clear and casual tone, emphasizing key points, in a manner that just feels like I am telling a story. My slides hardly contain any words and are driven mostly by images that complement what I say. I take them through the Hero's Journey of the entrepreneurs, and I invite them to also take their own Hero's Journey with me as we move forward.

Chapter 6: Pitching to Anyone, Anywhere

Pitching to venture capitalists

Going back to my pitch to Franco, he was very clear with his goals. 'At the end of the day, I have over seventy limited partners (LPs) who've invested in the fund. As a VC I am answerable to my LPs, and if I don't show the returns within the time horizon I promised, I get called out,' he shared with me. 'More importantly as a VC,' Franco adds, 'what is my potential exit?'

This made me ponder on some things. Now that I'm set to go down this path as a 'growth business' instead of a 'lifestyle business,' I need to also think of my own exit strategy, which I've been ruminating on for weeks.

I've researched the closest media properties to what we're doing—*The Voice*, *The Apprentice*, *Shark Tank*. The closest model, though, is done by Simon Cowell with his Got Talent Franchise. His deals with Sony Music, wherein they were able to jointly scale their media properties around the world, were the closest thing to what I was trying to do.

All of a sudden, it became clear.

Chapter 7: Valuation and Due Diligence

Due diligence and the data room

We're currently in the process of preparing our Data Room. We have all Securities and Exchange Commission documents, financial statements, including our trademark with the Intellectual Property Office for *The Final Pitch*.

The NDA

The NDA is a legally binding contract where the party or parties signing the agreement agree that sensitive information they obtain will not be made available to any others. As my legal counsel Mark Gorriceta has said in Chapter 7, 'Depending on the stage of the negotiation and extent of information to be shared, non-competition and/or non-Solicitation clauses may also be added to an NDA'.

The term sheet

As our non-binding term sheet is being prepared, the idea is to be able to have the investors give an indication of how much of what we are offering they intend to take up. The ideal scenario is for the round to be oversubscribed, and to choose to accept funding from the most ideal and strategic investors. I already have a short list of who I want onboard, but paranoia is making me want to make the list longer. I think I will choose the latter.

Arriving at your valuation

Since we are a revenue stage company, our consultant, Filbert Tsai of Equity Labs, came up with a table on how to justify our valuation. Apart from the numbers, however, I feel our story, track record and vision is the big intangible that makes our value even bigger than that.

Chapter 8: Insights from Around the World

Of all the insights and advice I've received, one thing that stands out at this point in time is the advice given to me by the legendary Tim Draper:

> 'It is important to use your current country to test your product in, but once you have the customer product fit, you should be thinking globally. Make sure your product or service is the best in the world, not just the best in your region. Also, I recommend thinking long and hard about the business model and how you are going to delight your customer.'

Tonight is the deadline for this book's manuscript, and I am submitting it not knowing how my next pitches will fare. It is one of the most exciting and terrifying things I will ever do in my life because I am expecting myself to succeed. Failure is not an option. Will I be able to raise the funding for our seed round? And even bigger money for our future expansion down the road? Find out what happens to the rest of the journey in this live document:

TheFinalPitch.ph/conclusion

Acknowledgement

If there is anything that any creative person can be gifted, it is that supportive and opposing force that allows one to pursue as much as reassess any major thought, decision and life direction. To my wife and business partner, Monica, thank you for always being the ear to which I pitch my crazy ideas. You have always been the conscientious and supportive life partner who has enabled me to follow my why. You have kept our household intact and risked your sanity to make sure all our family's needs were met during the pandemic. I love you.

To our children Danielle, Luis and David, may you find your own individual paths to happiness in whatever you end up doing. Pursue your passions with vigour, treat people kindly and remember to always dream big.

Six months into the pandemic, Penguin Random House SEA's Publisher Nora Abu Bakar reached out to work with me on this book. Amazingly, we have never even met, but I thank technology and her for finding me and allowing my voice to be heard by a much bigger audience. To my editor Amberdawn Manaois, your level of insight and elegance in exposition is just what we needed to make the book a more organized and compelling read.

I could not even begin to imagine writing and finishing this book without the help of my writing and research team, Annelle Juego and

Carla Bauto Deña. Thank you for being with me for every interview across time zones, and for every word of the manuscript. As always, our office manager, Leng Bulabos, for being my reliable mother hen who is always on top of everything.

I interviewed over fifty people for this book, and I wish to thank them all individually for their time, knowledge, and wisdom. They are:

1. Jeffrey Seah, partner at Quest Ventures
2. Mark Gorriceta, managing partner at Gorriceta Africa Cauton & Saavedra
3. Doron Latzer, founder of and senior partner at Pearl Cohen
4. Ronster Baetiong, co-founder and CEO of Podcast Network Asia
5. Josef Acuna, co-founder and chief content and operations officer of Podcast Network Asia
6. Jojo Flores, co-founder of Plug and Play Tech Centre
7. William Bao Bean, general partner at SOSV and managing director of Chinaccelerator and MOX
8. Roland Ros, co-founder of Kumu
9. Christopher Peralta, founder of Silicon Valley HQ
10. Earl Valencia, co-founder and Chief Business Officer of Plentina
11. Mohan Belani, co-founder and CEO of e27
12. Anuj Jain, co-founder and CEO of Startup-O
13. Carlo Calimon, director at Startup Village
14. Paul Rivera, co-founder and CEO of Kalibrr
15. Vincent Lau, co-founder and CEO of Maria Health
16. David Lang, founder and CEO of Viettonkin Joint Stock Company
17. Mario Berta, country managing director of Igloo Insure and co-founder of FlySpaces
18. David Beckett, author of Pitch to Win and creator of The Pitch Canvas©
19. Jacqueline van den Ende, co-founder of Carbon Equity
20. Mica Tan, CEO of MFT Group of Companies Inc.
21. Brian Ngan, venture partner at VU Venture Partners

22. Enrique Soriano III, executive director at Wong + Bernstein Advisory Group

23. Steve Sy, founder and CEO of Great Deals E-Commerce Corp.

24. Pascal Finette, co-founder of be radical

25. Jeffrey Rogers, principal, Learning and Facilitation at be radical

26. Supachai 'Kid' Parchariyanon, co-founder and CEO of RISE - Corporate Innovation Powerhouse

27. Katrina Rausa Chan, executive director at QBO

28. Patrick and Alex Gentry, founders of Sprout Solutions

29. Amra Naidoo, co-founder of and general partner at Accelerating Asia

30. Chelsea Krost, American author and leading millennial influencer in the US

31. Ashley Smithers, founder of and principal at 1821 Design Studio

32. Dov Moran, tech innovator, investor and world-renowned inventor of the USB flash drive

33. Filbert Richerd Ng Tsai, managing director at Equity Labs

34. Paula Rizzo, Emmy Award-winning TV producer and media strategist

35. Jessica Chen, Emmy Award-winning keynote speaker and founder and CEO of Soulcast Media

36. Warren Leow, Group CEO of Inmagine

37. Michael Dargani, CEO of Ananta Industries, Inc. and IceDream, Inc.

38. Victor Chua, founding and managing partner at Vynn Capital

39. Inbal Arieli, author of 'Chutzpah: Why Israel is a Hub of Innovation and Entrepreneurship'

40. Matthijs Geert-Jan van Leeuwen, director at Sunway iLabs

41. Leticia Souza, vice president of Finance at SAVii

42. Tim Draper, founding partner of venture capital firm Draper Fisher Jurvetson

43. Artie Lopez, co-founder of and startup coach at Brainsparks

44. Ben Ampil, US-certified neuro linguistic programming trainer and neurocoach

45. Jose 'Caya' Cayasso, co-founder and CEO of Slidebean

46. Ray Refundo, founder and CEO of Qwikwire
47. Joseph de Leon, founder of Manila Angel Investors Network
48. Ambassador Benedicto Yujuico, president of the Philippine Chamber of Commerce Industry
49. Josh Aragon, co-founder and CEO of Zagana
50. Rovilson Fernandez, writer, producer, and TV show host
51. Mori Rodriguez, chief innovation officer of the EON Group
52. Patrick Grove, co-founder and CEO of Catcha Group

I would like to acknowledge all of our investor judges on *The Final Pitch* from day one, who trusted us with the show. Jose 'Jomag' Magsaysay, Henry Lim Bon Liong, Mica Tan, Mikee Romero, Michael Dargani, Jet Yu, Dino Araneta, Mark Vernon, William Tiu Lim, Cesar Wee, Cary Lagdameo, Victor Consunji, George Royeca, Li Hao Zhuang, Vince Yamat, Joel Santos, John Januszczak, Dennis Anthony Uy, David Almirol, Rose Ong, Bernard Dy and Jay Villarante.

To all our show's past mentors, thank you for lending your knowledge and expertise. The late Edmo Morato and Tomy Lopez, Jay Bernardo, Andy Ferreria, Mon Jocson, Kenneth Cobonpue, Amor Maclang, Joey Gotuaco, Lito Lucas, Tristan de Belloy, Dowan Kim, Raul M. Castro, Akarsh Dhaiya, Rock Cleo, Alex Cabrera, Vikki Luta, Filbert Tsai, Paul Rivera, Kat Manalo, Junie del Mundo, Hardy Lipana, Julius dela Cruz, Patt Soyao, Yasmin Neri-Soyao and Dean Bernales.

Our awesome production team led by Adonis 'The Don' Pira, ably backed up by Eugene Gonzales, Khai Faune, Jun Barlis, Leanne Gili, and our hardworking and dedicated crew.

A+E Networks/History Channel's Leslie Castañeda, Riley Leong, and the rest of the team for airing our first season of the show.

The CNN Philippines team for always being a trusted broadcast partner. Tek Ramos-Major, Michi Ancheta, Gerald Ayuson, and Rico Hizon for all the promotional interviews on *The Final Word*.

Special thanks to GoNegosyo Founder Joey Concepcion for providing the inspiration for *The Final Pitch*.

To all the entrepreneurs and startups we have worked with on the show, thank you for being part of our collective nation-building efforts.

Bibliography

1. David Beckett's Pitch Canvas©. https://best3minutes.com/the-pitch-canvas
2. Armstrong, B. (26 December 2018). 'How Exercise Affects Your Brain.' Retrieved from https://www.scientificamerican.com/article/how-exercise-affects-your-brain/
3. Keefe, P. (27 December 2018). 'How Mark Burnett Resurrected Donald Trump as an Icon of American Success.' *The New Yorker*. Retrieved from https://www.newyorker.com/magazine/2019/01/07/how-mark-burnett-resurrected-donald-trump-as-an-icon-of-american-success
4. University of Washington's faculty resource. https://faculty.washington.edu/ejslager/random-generator/index.html